D0725903

Managing Knowledge
to Fuel Growth

The Results-Driven Manager Series

The Results-Driven Manager series collects timely articles from *Harvard Management Update*, *Harvard Management Communication Letter*, and the *Balanced Scorecard Report* to help senior to middle managers sharpen their skills, increase their effectiveness, and gain a competitive edge. Presented in a concise, accessible format to save managers valuable time, these books offer authoritative insights and techniques for improving job performance and achieving immediate results.

Other books in the series:

A Timesaving Guide

THE RESULTS-DRIVEN MANAGER

Managing Knowledge to Fuel Growth

• • •

Harvard Business School Press

Boston, Massachusetts

Copyright 2007 Harvard Business School Publishing Corporation
All rights reserved
Printed in the United States of America
11 10 09 08 07   5 4 3 2 1

No part of this publication may be reproduced, stored in or introduced
into a retrieval system, or transmitted, in any form, or by any means
(electronic, mechanical, photocopying, recording, or otherwise),
without the prior permission of the publisher. Requests for permission
should be directed to permissions@hbsp.harvard.edu, or mailed to
Permissions, Harvard Business School Publishing, 60 Harvard Way,
Boston, Massachusetts 02163.

Library of Congress Cataloging-in-Publication Data

Managing knowledge to fuel growth.
     p. cm.—(the results-driven manager series)
   ISBN-13: 978-1-4221-1468-1 (pbk. : alk. paper)
   ISBN-10: 1-4221-1468-6
   1. Knowledge management.   2. Knowledge workers.
3. Personnel management.   4. Information technology.
I. Harvard Business School Press.
   HD30.2.M3655 2007
   658.4'038—dc22   2007000883

Contents

Contents

Managing Knowledge in Your Team

Managing Leaders' Knowledge

Introduction

. . .

More than 30 years ago, management guru Peter Drucker declared: "To make knowledge work productive will be the great management task of this century, just as to make manual work productive was the great management task of the last century." Drucker's instincts about making knowledge work productive—that is, managing knowledge—were spot-on.

But what exactly is knowledge—and for that matter, what's knowledge management? A company's knowledge takes numerous forms, including information and learning that employees have acquired through carrying out their jobs, as well as the unique skills and capabilities embodied in the workforce that give the company a competitive advantage. Knowledge can also take the form of information in databases, reports, and manuals, along with intellectual property (patents, copyrights, trademarks, trade secrets, and so forth) that the company possesses and that is afforded legal protection.

Knowledge *management* (KM) entails first figuring out what information a company possesses (in all its forms) that could benefit the organization. Then it means devising ways of making that information easily available to the people who can turn it into valuable products, services, and processes. KM practices vary across companies but often involve:

- Creating repositories of information about best practices

- Setting up networks for transferring information between employees who interact with customers and those who create the company's products or services

- Creating formal procedures to ensure that lessons learned in the course of a project get passed along to others doing similar tasks

- Drawing on informal networks of people who have been at the organization for a long time and who can connect those in need of specific information with those who can provide it

Managers who excel at KM generate impressive results for their organizations, including:

- PRODUCTIVITY GAINS: For instance, by studying and sharing key processes in each of its wafer-fabrication plants, Texas Instruments got the equivalent yield of one plant out of its existing facilities in just six months—fast enough to meet market changes. And Ford Motor Company's so-called Best Practice Replication system helped plant managers achieve the companywide objective of 5% annual productivity improvements.

- COST SAVINGS: For example, oil giant Chevron saved more than $650 million between 1991 and 1999 by sharing best practices among managers in charge of energy use at its refineries. Meanwhile, Texas Instruments saved more than $1 billion by disseminating best practices through-out its 13 semiconductor plants—which enabled it to avoid the expense of constructing an entirely new plant.

- A KEENER COMPETITIVE EDGE: To illustrate, one large consumer-goods company was able to offer its products to customers more quickly, cheaply, efficiently, and innovatively than rival compa-nies could after it established a formal knowl-edge management system. In addition, professional services provider Ernst & Young enabled its consultants to develop proposals faster—and therefore win more business—by compiling "PowerPack" document collections containing information tailored to specific industries.

Clearly, managing knowledge can pay big dividends. Indeed, conventional wisdom holds out KM as "the single most valuable corporate asset in the 21st century," maintains business writer Mattison Crowe, and "this capability will become increasingly important." Echoing these sentiments, management expert Charles Handy estimates the value of a company's knowledge (which Handy calls intellectual capital) at three to four times the book value of the firm's tangible assets. Other estimates spiral upward from there.

Why has knowledge management become so crucial? The experts offer several explanations. For one thing, says Tom Davenport, President's Distinguished Professor of Information Technology & Management at Babson, knowledge workers now constitute the majority of employees in advanced economies. These employees have a high degree of education or expertise, and their work primarily involves the creation, distribution, or application of knowledge. "Their activity—which includes R&D, marketing, engineering, planning, customer service, and management—is critical to [their company's] innovation and growth," Davenport explains. Companies that fail to manage such workers' knowledge risk missing out on the crucial benefits that effective KM promises.

Moreover, demographic changes—an impending wave of retirements among aging workers as well as increased turnover among employees of all ages—hint at trouble ahead for organizations everywhere. According to Accenture partners David Boath and David Y. Smith, these changes suggest that companies are facing "an ongoing, irreplaceable loss of the knowledge, experience, and wisdom that have been a primary source of [their] competitiveness and profitability." And this "brain drain" will likely get worse as ever larger waves of Baby Boomers leave the workforce to settle into retirement.

"For a business to compete successfully in the new millennium, it's . . . going to need better access to its potential brainpower," says Crowe. So how can companies retain and build on the great body of knowledge represented by their workforces? It isn't easy. Managers seeking to develop and implement KM strategies can expect to encounter numerous obstacles and pitfalls. For example, knowledge workers do not constitute a monolithic group: The information and skills they possess differ widely, as do the ways in which their knowledge can best be leveraged for the benefit of their organization. Thus KM strategies must be tailored to the specific types of knowledge in question—which can be a daunting task.

In addition, too many managers mistakenly "think [that] technology is the great fix for all knowledge [management] woes," says Carla O'Dell, who studied Texas Instruments' KM practices while writing a book on the subject. Such managers assume that, to manage their firms' knowledge, they merely need to "put up a database" and "[have] everyone put their stuff in it." "If you build it," explains O'Dell, "they will not [necessarily] come, [nor will] they . . . add their stuff—and then the first few people who visit it looking for answers don't find any. And that's the end of the story."

Owing to these and other difficulties, many organizations' KM initiatives start with a bang and end with a whimper. Indeed, most knowledge management programs risk never advancing beyond the pilot phase. Yet with some careful thought and program design, you *can* boost your odds of designing effective KM strategies for your own team, unit, or division. The articles in this volume provide a wealth of practical guidelines and potent tools. Here's a quick preview of what you'll find in the pages that follow.

Why Knowledge Management?

The articles in this section define knowledge management in detail, shed light on why KM is increasingly important for companies, and examine the obstacles and pitfalls managers can expect to encounter while establishing KM systems. These selections also provide additional insights related to the design of companywide KM strategies.

For example, the first selection—"Do We Know How to Do That?"—presents guidelines for determining whether a formal KM system is right for your company overall. The answer is "yes" if your organization operates in several locations, or if it has just one location but employs more than several hundred people. Common mistakes to avoid include launching an overly large, complex KM initiative; relying too much on technological shortcuts; neglecting to demonstrate knowledge management in your own on-the-job behavior; and failing to reward people for sharing knowledge.

"Knowledge Management: Four Obstacles to Overcome" focuses on additional errors many companies make while setting up a KM system. For example, some managers treat KM as an end in itself rather than using it to address specific business problems. Others focus their attention only on the KM pilot project but forget about the rollout. As their attention shifts from KM to other concerns, resources for the rollout dry up. Still other managers don't clarify the specific tasks needed to ensure a KM initiative's success, nor do they articulate who will be responsible for each task and who will "own" each initiative. Finally, too many managers take a one-size-fits-all approach to KM—even though knowledge management systems work best when they're tailored to individual users' needs and to the unique characteristics of their work.

In "Can You Boost Knowledge Work's Impact on the Bottom Line?" Tom Davenport specifically addresses this issue of customization in developing effective KM practices. "The key to improving productivity [of your knowledge workers] is to tailor the intervention to the type of work," he maintains. To illustrate, for "transaction" workers (such as call center representatives), it's helpful to "script" the work using databases and work-flow automation tools. "Call center reps are often told what to say under every circumstance and in response to every imaginable customer comment or question," Davenport explains. "Access to knowledge resources is tightly constrained by the need for heads-down productivity and responsiveness to customers; there isn't the time to search through a repository." But you wouldn't use these same practices with "collaborative" workers, such as internal consultants with deep expertise who work across multiple functions. Their job processes involve too much uncertainty to be scripted. Such workers "are best served by a series of tools they can draw upon as needed; the individual worker [not the company] remains the integrator of the tools and knowledge."

In "Intellectual Capital for the Perplexed," business writer Mattison Crowe maintains that an organization's knowledge becomes valuable only through the interplay of three types of intellectual capital: 1) *human capital* (such as unique skills around which your organization has built its business), 2) *structural capital* (including intellectual property, company goals and strategies, and information systems), and 3) *customer capital* (your firm's customers, suppliers, and market channels, as well as the industry associations, trade groups, and government policymakers with whom your company interacts).

Crowe also describes tools for measuring, capturing, and exploiting your firm's intellectual capital. These tools include competency maps (which describe the skills and attributes employees need to do their jobs successfully), communities of practice (groups of employees who meet regularly to share knowledge and who are informally bound to one another through exposure to a common set of problems), and corporate "yellow pages" (an index of experts in your organization by field of inquiry). Additional tools are lessons databases (data warehouses of key lessons archived for future reference) and knowledge forums (online spaces where your company's employees, customers, and suppliers can interact).

The final article in this section is "When Your Best People Leave, Will Their Knowledge Leave, Too?" by Accenture partners David Boath and David Y. Smith. The authors focus on the demographic changes driving the departure of knowledgeable and experienced employees from the workforce and the costs of this "brain drain" for companies. Boath and Smith also introduce suggestions for retaining and building on the knowledge embodied in your workforce. For instance, identify the knowledge that's most crucial for your company's strategy *and* most at risk for being lost. Then institutionalize that knowledge; for example, by interviewing these individuals to articulate precisely what they do at the company and then documenting that information. Better succession planning and adoption of advanced e-learning techniques can further help you retain knowledge.

Managing Knowledge in Your Team

The articles in this section concentrate on how to manage knowledge in your team, department, or division. In "Knowledge Management: Four Practical Steps," consultant Diane McFerrin Peters advocates creating a setting that fosters the sharing of knowledge. For example, consider establishing an open meeting policy, by which everyone can attend any meeting. Furnish conference rooms with round tables, "so no one can sit at the head and dictate discussions." Also allow people to skip hierarchical levels in sharing ideas with you and other higher-ups: Your group will generate more ideas on how to do things better. And have people keep track of how much time they typically spend on various activities. Decide whether day-to-day activity supports your group's ability to develop, apply, and share ideas. If not, outsource or end activities unrelated to these priorities.

"Managing Knowledge: How to Make Money with What You Know" describes a six-step process for putting together a successful KM program for a team or unit: 1) *Define the program's purpose.* For example, do you want to increase customer intimacy? Accelerate time to market? Enhance operational excellence? 2) *Choose a process.* Will you provide database technology and let employees use it to find the information they need? Will you encourage the use of "knowledge networks"—groups of individuals who can share what they've learned through various projects? 3) *Find and enlist the right people*, including individuals who have experience leading change efforts. 4) *Ensure that technology supports your data.* 5) *Invest in training knowledge workers.* 6) *Focus your KM effort on your group's strategy.*

In addition, this selection provides a special sidebar on learning histories—storytelling that helps to codify the tacit knowledge of an organization that would otherwise get lost. To compile learning histories, people gather in study groups to tell their own stories about projects that have been both successes and failures.

In "Debriefing Gabriel Szulanski: Improving Best-Practice Transfer," business writer Lauren Keller Johnson interviews Gabriel Szulanski, professor of strategy at INSEAD. Johnson shares Szulanski's knowledge of how managers can overcome employees' resistance to transferring best practices from their team to other teams. According to Szulanski, people have several reasons for resisting sharing knowledge about best practices. For example, some don't think that a best practice will be effective in a new situation. Others don't recognize the value of new knowledge, or they lack the shared language to put that knowledge to work in other departments. Still others don't have a history of positive communication and collaboration with peers elsewhere in the organization.

Szulanski then explains how to "unstick" knowledge despite these barriers. For example, he recommends doing whatever it takes to forge bonds between people in different departments. "In intimate relationships," he says, "people feel invested in those bonds. They enjoy interacting, they collaborate quickly and more productively, and they're more responsive to each other. All this is essential in best-practice transfer—because the two parties must interact repeatedly over long periods of time."

But knowledge about what works best for specific groups in an organization isn't the only valuable type of information you should capture and share. You also want to obtain data about your company's rivals and ensure that your people use it to improve your own group's performance. "The Power of Competitive Intelligence," by business writer David Stauffer, examines this subject. Stauffer offers four suggestions: 1) *Collect the data* on your competitors—information that often can be obtained from rivals' employees and other stakeholders. 2) *Give meaning to the data*—by evaluating what you've learned in light of economic conditions, customer attitudes, potential regulatory actions, and other forces in the larger environment. 3) *Connect the data to your bottom line*. For example, if you've heard that a rival company has some unhappy customers, how might you use that information to capture those customers and thereby boost your own firm's revenues? 4) *Organize the effort*. For example, consider outsourcing competitive intelligence assignments to consultants who can attend trade shows and learn more about your rivals without revealing your company's name to these competitors.

In "Debriefing Thomas Davenport: Are You Getting the Most from Your Knowledge Workers?" Lauren Keller

Johnson shares Davenport's insights about how managers must redefine their role in order to extract maximum value from their knowledge workers. In particular, managers need to move from acting like "bosses" to acting like "players and coaches." They must be able to perform knowledge work similar to that performed by their subordinates, and they need to protect their knowledge workers from bureaucracy. Examples of this protection include ensuring that adequate funds flow into the right knowledge-work projects, translating the content of knowledge work for other managers who don't understand it, and parrying attempts to impose unnecessary structure on knowledge workers.

Managing Leaders' Knowledge

Leaders' knowledge and experience play a unique role in a company's performance. Thus, developing—and then managing—what they know requires unique strategies. The articles in this section examine this subject.

In "What the Chief Learning Officer Actually Knows," business writer Loren Gary writes that many companies have created a new type of leader to help transform intellectual assets into enduring value for an organization's customers and employees. This new executive—chief learning officer, or CLO—may also be called chief knowledge officer or director of knowledge management. He or she is not to be confused with the chief information officer (CIO) or chief technology officer (CTO). Unlike these other executives, the CLO ensures that the organization has the processes, the systems, and the culture to facilitate effective knowledge sharing—both within the organization and between the organization and its customers. Gary then presents principles and practices that an effective CLO applies—such as distinguishing between "know that," "know why," and "know how" types of knowledge and treating them differently.

In "The Art of Developing Leaders," Bain & Company consultants Vijay Vishwanath and Marcia Blenko describe the strategies that Kraft Foods has used to develop many corporate managers and executives. The authors then identify lessons that other companies can learn from Kraft's experience. Kraft's remarkably successful approach to developing leaders comprises five guiding principles: 1) Give up-and-comers bottom-line responsibility early on. 2) Once young managers have mastered the basics of the business, give them broad leeway in deciding how to meet their targets. 3) School managers in the art of exercising influence, not issuing orders. 4) Encourage collective achievement, not self-promotion. 5) Commit to retaining talented people.

The final article in this section—"Five Questions About Peer-to-Peer Leadership Development"—presents insights from CompanyCommand.com. This Web site serves as a professional forum for U.S. Army officers at the first level of command authority. The goal of CompanyCommand .com is to create a community of practice that provides those who are in the middle of a leadership challenge with real-time connections to peers who have had similar experiences. Four Army majors, along with a knowledge-management consultant, provide examples of how this community of practice has helped Army officers not only enhance their knowledge with the help of peers but also strengthen their effectiveness as leaders.

Leveraging Knowledge Management Technology

As the article about CompanyCommand.com makes clear, technology can play a vital role in knowledge management. But technology in itself isn't enough; companies must use it effectively. The articles in this section examine this theme more closely.

"The New Uses of Intranets" sets the stage by defining the benefits that a company intranet—its Web-based knowledge-management system—can generate. An intranet facilitates training and knowledge sharing, including interactive and distance learning. For instance, at retailer JCPenney, a manager can sign in to the site and then view a desktop customized to his or her function and level. The desktop contains training programs and management tips. Indeed, the company no longer publishes or mails training materials—which is a huge savings for a far-flung retailer that hires between 400 and 700 management trainees a year. In addition to providing easy access to information and enabling cost savings, intranets help companies automate routine tasks as well as organize and communicate data.

In "The Right Data at the Right Fingertips," consultant Frank Steinfield presents a case study of how companies have used Web technology to manage knowledge. Krispy Kreme, for example, created its dynamic KM portal (mykrispykreme.com) to compile and redistribute time-sensitive operational data. The technology has enabled the company's "ultrafast deployment of new outposts"—as well as helped it expand revenues and cut costs. Steinfield offers several suggestions for building a KM portal. For instance, build the system on a technology platform that's already familiar to the workforce. That way, people will find it easier to use the new system—and therefore will be more likely to embrace it.

Finally, in "Communication Technology That's Worth a Second Look," consultant Eric Marcus explains how to get the most from your KM technology. For example, while many companies have had difficulty getting more than a handful of employees to invest effort in KM systems, some firms have found ways to address this challenge. According to Marcus, a major European bank "changed the front end of its intranet to a graphical interface that looked like a village. Buildings reflected the various aspects of the bank's business. Within each building, lobby marquees identified what 'discussions' were taking place on each floor, and then, on each floor marquees identified the 'discussions' going on in each room. All employees were invited to see and experience the village."

"Initially," writes Marcus, "employees visited the [revised] intranet just to see what all the talk was about. Then use began to grow. Soon, employees indicated that their primary motivation for going to the intranet was the sense of achievement they got from solving problems, in many cases with people they had never met."

As you read the articles that follow, consider how you might respond to the following questions:

- How does your company currently manage knowledge? How does your team, department, or division manage knowledge? What has worked well about your company's and team's current approaches to KM? What could be improved?

- Which of the common pitfalls to KM (if any) have you fallen victim to? For example, do you tend to pay more attention to KM pilot projects than to such projects' rollout phase? How might you avoid such pitfalls in the future?

- What knowledge is *most* essential to sustaining or strengthening your company's competitive position? Who in your firm or unit possesses that knowledge? What could you do to retain those individuals and make the most of their

expertise? How might you codify their knowledge so that others in the company can leverage
it—even if those individuals were to leave the
organization?

- How do you develop leaders' knowledge in your
  unit? If your company does not have a chief
  learning officer, how might you perform some
  of the same functions as a CLO?

- In what ways does your company or unit use
  technology (such as online learning and Web-
  based communities of practice) to manage
  knowledge? How useful has that technology
  been? In what ways might you improve KM
  technology's value to your organization? How
  might you encourage employees to use the
  technology, if they're currently resisting
  doing so?

Why Knowledge Management?

• • •

What makes knowledge management (KM) so crucial to organizations today? In the articles that follow, you'll find answers to this question—including detailed definitions of KM, examples of why it has become increasingly important for companies, and descriptions of the obstacles and pitfalls managers can expect to encounter while establishing KM systems. These selections also provide insights related to the design of companywide KM strategies.

Do We Know How to Do That?

Understanding Knowledge Management

· · ·

The phrase *"knowledge management"* has been buzzing around for a while now, and knowledge-management programs have been launched at countless companies during the last few years. So you have doubtless heard the words more times than you care to remember. Despite the beliefs of elementary-school teachers everywhere, however, repetition does not always beget understanding. What are we really talking about here?

What It Is

Knowledge management is a formal, directed process of figuring out what information a company has that could benefit others in the company, then devising ways of making it easily available. Practices vary from one organization to another, but often involve such steps as:

- creating repositories of information about best practices,

- setting up networks for transferring information between employees who interact with customers and those who create the product, and

- creating formal procedures to ensure that lessons learned in the course of a project are passed along to others doing similar tasks.

Without such steps, what passes for knowledge management is informal and haphazard. A team working on a task runs into difficulties. Members ask around to see if anyone else has done similar work, and whether that person has any suggestions or advice. Sometimes this pays off. But because there's rarely an easy way to find out who has worked on what, the process is time-consuming, and the results are a matter of luck. The knowledge that has accumulated in the company may never be discovered or passed along.

Formal knowledge management can prevent this waste of time and resources, which is why it has been adopted by corporations such as British Petroleum, Monsanto, PricewaterhouseCoopers, Hewlett-Packard, and many others. The results are often spectacular. Chevron calculates that it has saved more than $650 million since 1991 by sharing best practices among managers in charge of energy use at its oil refineries. A knowledge-management program helped Texas Instruments save more than $1 billion by disseminating best practices throughout its 13 semiconductor plants.

Texas Instruments' experience illustrates how the process works. The company's semiconductor markets were booming, but it was reluctant to build a costly new fabrication plant given the mercurial nature of the industry. "Because those markets change quickly . . . if you can't produce while the customer is hot, you're missing out," explains Carla O'Dell, who studied TI while writing a new book on knowledge management. So TI's challenge was to learn to produce more and different types of semiconductors without building another plant.

Tom Engibous, then head of the semiconductor division and now CEO of the company, told his managers that they needed to get the equivalent yield of another wafer fabrication plant out of their existing facilities. "[He said,] 'Some of you are good at one thing and some of you are good at another, and we've got the data to show it. So we've got to find a way to transfer those best practices fast,'" says O'Dell, who is also president of

American Productivity and Quality Council (APQC), a nonprofit organization that helps companies learn from the best practices of others. Because sharing knowledge runs counter to the instincts of most managers, Engibous changed the incentive system for plant managers: instead of compensation based on the yield of their own plants, they would now be rewarded based on the collective yield of all the plants.

Thus incented, the managers got busy. They assembled teams to study the key processes in each plant. The teams figured out the best way to do a task, collated the information, and took it back to their own plants. Thanks to these efforts, the company was able to hit its yield goal in six months—fast enough to meet changes in the market, and three months less than the time required to build a new plant. Adds O'Dell: "They have done it twice more and say they've saved $1.5 billion as a result."

Is It Appropriate for Your Organization?

While savings like those of Chevron and Texas Instruments can only be achieved by giant multinationals, all reasonably large companies or business units may be able to make impressive productivity gains through a formal knowledge-management system. How large do you need to be? According to Chuck Sieloff, knowledge-management program manager at Hewlett-Packard, the "clearest breakpoint" is companies with multiple locations, which invariably need a formal program. As for companies with only one location, "I don't know exactly where the breakpoint is, but once you get above several hundred people you no longer automatically know what's going on and who knows what."

Size is only the first step in ascertaining whether your company or unit could benefit from knowledge management. A second step, says Sieloff, is assessing your company's culture regarding knowledge, so that you know what may need changing. "Start by asking yourself why the knowledge isn't [now] being shared. In some companies it's a cultural issue, where people don't feel that they're rewarded to share knowledge. They basically feel they're better off not doing that." Of course, you also need to know what doesn't need changing. At some companies, for example, informal networks already do an effective job of managing knowledge. "It's the 'six degrees of separation' phenomenon," says Sieloff. "If you have a culture that has a lot of informal networks and people who have been around for a long time—like in our company turnover is very low—you can rely a little more on 'Do you know someone who knows someone?'"

Mark G. Mazzie, chief knowledge officer for the consulting firm Barnett International, agrees that it's often possible to avoid reinventing the wheel in this process. "While you're ultimately trying to change the culture of an organization, you don't want to make it doubly hard by introducing a new infrastructure or a new way of communicating when one already exists. Often there is some method that already exists. . . . You just have to make it more user-friendly."

Implementation

If you decide that there's a need for a formal knowledge-management program, the next step is to conduct a formal audit of what your company needs to know and where that knowledge might be found. According to APQC's O'Dell, this involves answering five questions:

- What processes in our organization have the biggest impact on the bottom line?

- What knowledge, if we had it, would make those processes work more effectively?

- Is this knowledge something we have inside the organization but don't get to the right places at the right times? Or is it knowledge we're going to have to go outside to acquire?

- Who would use the knowledge?

- How do we start bringing knowledge to people?

One multinational company O'Dell worked with, for example, was in the process of changing its business model from selling products to selling customized solutions. Going through the five questions, people from the organization determined that the process with the biggest impact on the bottom line was the sales process itself. Then they asked the people involved in selling what would help them sell more effectively in the new environment. The salespeople responded that they wanted to know whether someone had sold a given solution before in another country—and if so, what industry they sold it to, what the solution looked like, and who they could call to find out more details.

Following up on these answers, the company discovered it had this information but wasn't utilizing it: each national unit had a database of solutions and approaches, but the databases were neither linked together nor shared. To jump-start a new approach, the company put together a task force of representatives from those units; their job was to figure out what information they needed to get to the salespeople and how they planned to go about it.

Avoiding Pitfalls

Knowledge-management programs founder on many rocks. Among the most dangerous obstacles identified by the experts are the following:

Starting Too Big

Knowledge sharing is an "unnatural act," says O'Dell— which is why it's wise to start small, preferably with pilot projects in which results can be measured in six to nine months. When it's time to gear up, though, expect to devote substantial resources—and aim for substantial gains. "If you want big results, it's going to be a direct function of how much you put into it. So don't pick something that doesn't matter if you don't improve it." Throughout the process, moreover, you need to be sure that someone's in charge. "[You need] a team leader who keeps things moving all the way through. It takes project management just like anything else."

Relying on Technological Shortcuts

Too often, people think technology is the great fix for all knowledge woes, says O'Dell. "A great predictor of failure is, the first thing you do is put up a database. 'Let's put up a database and everyone put their stuff in it.' If you build it, they will not come, they won't add their stuff—and then the first few people who visit it looking for answers don't find any. And that's the end of the story. Then you've polluted the waters for the next time you want to put fish in it." Adds Anne Stuart, managing editor at *CIO* Magazine: "Companies that simply stockpile data with little organization and no analysis often find that, given strains on storage space and the time wasted looking for misplaced materials, too much information is worse than none at all."

In fact, Bob Guns of PricewaterhouseCoopers' knowledge-management practice area says you should consider putting some types of information everywhere *but* in a database. "Identify the best practices in the organization and collect anecdotal data," he advises. "Have those written up by professional writers, and have them embedded in all kinds of places . . . in training programs, possibly in policies and procedures, . . . in as many different dimensions of the organization as possible." That way, people will encounter the information regularly, not just when they go looking for it.

Not Modeling the Behavior

If managers don't incorporate knowledge management into their own behavior, it won't work. One key, says Hewlett-Packard's Sieloff, is simply asking the right kinds of questions. Managers have to ask people whether they tried to leverage existing knowledge and how they're planning to share the knowledge they gained on the last project.

Ignoring the Power of Rewards

People who are rewarded for sharing knowledge do more of it. One technique is to incorporate knowledge management into formal performance evaluations and incentive-compensation systems, says Sieloff: "What needs to be turned around [is] that you will be recognized and rewarded for what you share, not for what you hoard." That means making sure that people who do share are singled out for recognition. It also means making sure their names are associated with the ideas they have contributed—that they become "famous" for what they have added to the company's knowledge base.

For Further Reading

Harvard Business Review on Knowledge Management (1998, Harvard Business School Press)

If Only We Knew What We Know: The Transfer of Internal Knowledge and Best Practice by Carla O'Dell and C. Jackson Grayson, Jr., with Nilly Essaides (1998, Free Press)

Intellectual Capital: The New Wealth of Organizations by Thomas A. Stewart (1997, Doubleday)

The Knowledge Evolution: Expanding Organizational Intelligence by Verna Allee (1997, Butterworth-Heinemann)

Working Knowledge: How Organizations Manage What They Know by Thomas H. Davenport and Laurence Prusak (1997, Harvard Business School Press)

Reprint U9902A

Knowledge Management

Four Obstacles to Overcome

· · ·

Knowledge management (KM) continues to be trendy and appealing—but so far it's a concept with a checkered career. A handful of organizations, such as the World Bank and Xerox Corp., have developed robust programs for sharing knowledge that are by now well integrated into everyday operations. But many others have launched initiatives that start with a bang and end with a whimper. According to American Productivity & Quality Center (APQC), which has conducted several studies of KM, most programs are in danger of getting stuck in the pilot phase.

Why so? Experts at APQC and elsewhere point to several potholes on the road to successful knowledge management. Among them are the following:

Lack of a Business Purpose

Too many companies treat KM as an end in itself, argues Nancy M. Dixon, a professor at George Washington University and author of the book *Common Knowledge: How Companies Thrive by Sharing What They Know*. They create a program because they think it will pay off later—or just because they think an effective organization should be able to share knowledge across departments.

That's exactly backward. "The goal is not to make knowledge management happen," says Dixon, "the goal is to deal with the organization's most pressing issues and to use KM where it's appropriate to do so." APQC president Carla O'Dell underscores the point. "The number-one reason KM initiatives may not function in an organization is that the 'evangelists' fail to connect with the real business issues," she says. "That's the pitfall of just trying to create vehicles for people to communicate and share—it's a solution looking for a problem."

Successful programs start with business problems that KM can help solve. Ernst & Young developed its "PowerPack" document collections—information tailored to specific industries—with the express goal of helping consultants develop proposals faster. Ford Motor Co.'s so-called Best Practice Replication system helps plant managers achieve the companywide objective of 5% annual productivity improvements. At Anadarko Petroleum, an oil exploration and production company, "everybody wants to bring in a new well," says planning analyst Tiffany Tyler. "That's such a buzz for people. And if we can show them we can cut cycle time by a week and make a better decision about where to drill the hole"—goals of the company's KM program—"it's, 'Well, don't you want to do that?' The answer is almost universally yes."

Poor Planning—and Inadequate Resources

Many companies focus their attention on the KM pilot project and forget about the rollout, says Richard McDermott, president of McDermott Consulting and a collaborator on some of the APQC studies. "Pilots, because they're new, get lots of attention and support. Senior managers see the pilot and think it's great—they'll lead the charge." Over time, though, key managers get transferred, the marketplace shifts, and attention is focused elsewhere. Pretty soon, resources have dried up.

To avoid this, McDermott advises planning the rollout at the same time you're launching the pilot. That allows managers to acknowledge (and plan for) the fact that "the real work comes after the pilot is done." It's important, too, to make sure that the company is prepared to

Measuring Progress

One sticky point about knowledge management (KM): it's tough to assess how you're doing. Tough, but not impossible. "Two things need to be tracked," says George Washington University professor Nancy M. Dixon: "an outcome measure and a process measure." The outcome measure depends on the objective you're trying to reach through better management of knowledge—increased productivity, faster turnaround time, whatever. "So long as KM is aimed toward a particular business goal," says Dixon, "it's possible to track it."

The process measure depends on the nature of your knowledge-management system. You want to know whether people are doing what you'd like them to do— tapping into the database, taking advantage of peer-assist consulting capabilities, putting designs into the design bank. It's hard to know when KM is "implemented," says Dixon. But you can know if people are doing the activities that you think of as knowledge management, and you can assess whether they're reaching the goals you're seeking.

commit real resources to the KM effort. "If you're going to start three pilots and you invest half a million to a million dollars in that, you ought to be thinking of a considerably larger investment in the overall rollout," says McDermott.

Best-practice companies don't hesitate to spend such sums. Many of the benchmark companies studied by

APQC laid out more than $1 million to get their programs started and spend more than that amount annually on ongoing development and maintenance. Ernst & Young, Dixon points out, spends a whopping 6% of revenue on knowledge management, though that figure includes technology investments that benefit KM but weren't designed exclusively for that purpose.

Lack of Accountability

Knowledge-management initiatives are likely to peter out unless responsibility for them is somebody's job. Big organizations may need several such somebodies. "There's a general rule of thumb: if you're a large corporation and you're trying to get started in this, you probably need four core people dedicated to it in addition to the IT people," says Carla O'Dell, who in addition to her APQC role is also coauthor of *If Only We Knew What We Know: The Transfer of Internal Knowledge and Best Practice.* Smaller companies can get by with one dedicated person, such as Anadarko's Tyler. But if no one's accountable for KM, it won't last.

The larger the initiative, the more people and job descriptions are required. Like many big professional-services firms, for example, Arthur Andersen has an extensive KM system, dubbed Knowledge Base. One thing that makes it work, says Andersen consultant W. Todd Huskinson, is the fact that literally hundreds of the firm's employees work on it—helping project managers elicit the lessons from their latest engagement, editing the content and keeping it fresh, even staffing a hotline to help consultants navigate the KM system. What's

> The number-one reason KM initiatives don't function? The "evangelists" fail to connect them with real business issues.

more, the firm's end-of-engagement checklist includes a question as to whether the deliverables and lessons were added to Knowledge Base. "So the partners and managers need to sign off on that: 'Yes, we've made a contribution based on this engagement.'"

Lack of Customization

Knowledge management is not a one-size-fits-all program. On the contrary: it works best when individual programs are tailored to the needs of individual users.

Ernst & Young's PowerPacks are designed for consultants in particular industries, points out Nancy Dixon. Chevron's Project Resources Group, a team of internal consultants with special areas of expertise, is a resource for managers of capital-intensive products. Knowledge-transfer systems, Dixon says, "are less useful and less effective when they are designed for just 'anyone' in the organization."

There's another way in which KM needs to be tailored: it needs to fit an organization's culture. A major requirement, according to one APQC study, is that it must be "tightly linked to a pre-existing core value of the organization." Two examples:

- At IBM's Lotus Development Corp. unit, there's a widespread feeling that Lotus "invented" collaborative technology—so "contributing ideas to a Lotus database and checking on the insights of others is simply how people do business at Lotus." Moreover, the Lotus culture is forgiving: projects don't have to be perfect the first time; "employees feel free to 'try things out' and modify what does not work." That's reflected in the way knowledge is shared.

- At Ford, the emphasis is on avoiding risk and getting it right. "Because Ford's development teams use an intranet Web site to communicate and to share knowledge within and among teams, their original documents, analyses, and discussions are available to senior managers. The opportunity to look at original work, rather than 'massaged' reports, builds on Ford's values of careful, complete, detailed analysis."

KM is still a young field; it's not surprising that so many organizations have only begun to implement it, nor that so many have bogged down. Still, they can learn from the pioneers. "Those that have been at it for a long time had to learn what they know by trial and error," says O'Dell. "But those that are coming into it are able to leapfrog over a lot of those early problems and make much faster progress."

For Further Reading

Common Knowledge: How Companies Thrive by Sharing What They Know by Nancy M. Dixon (2000, Harvard Business School Press)

If Only We Knew What We Know: The Transfer of Internal Knowledge and Best Practice by Carla O'Dell and C. Jackson Grayson, Jr., with Nilly Essaides (1998, Free Press)

Reprint U0008B

Can You Boost Knowledge Work's Impact on the Bottom Line?

• • •

Tom Davenport

More than 30 years ago, Peter Drucker declared: "To make knowledge work productive will be the great management task of this century, just as to make manual work productive was the great management task of the last century." Although we have yet to achieve this goal, there are good reasons to keep trying.

Knowledge workers are difficult to define and count, but they are undoubtedly a major component—perhaps a majority—of the U.S. and other advanced economies. I'd define them as people with a high degree of education or expertise whose work primarily involves the creation, distribution, or application of knowledge. Some knowledge workers have high levels of autonomy and discretion in how they do their work; others have more structured roles. Their activity—which includes R&D, marketing, engineering, planning, customer service, and management—is critical to innovation and growth.

Previous productivity-oriented programs, such as process reengineering and quality, didn't really take a cut at knowledge workers. How can we enhance our economy by increasing the speed and quality of our most valuable labor force? For starters, it's critical to point out what not to do.

A research project I conducted a few years ago originally focused on "reengineering knowledge work processes," but it became abundantly clear that the "r" word didn't apply. Managers of R&D and marketing departments acknowledged the need to improve processes, yet they cringed at the prospect of top-down, radical change. For whatever process you're redesigning, it's probably a good idea to include the workers in the redesign; it seemed particularly important to do this with autonomous, independent knowledge workers. My fellow researchers and I also realized that breaking down processes into detailed task flows wouldn't work: the knowledge workers we interviewed often felt that their work was too unpredictable and unstructured to be diagrammed on a flow chart. In short, few of the traditional process innovation or improvement approaches seemed to apply.

Technology has typically been viewed as having great potential to enhance knowledge work, but I've noticed a change over the past several years. When I first began to research knowledge work improvement initiatives, companies were beginning to implement knowledge repositories under the banner of "knowledge management." They were interested in capturing the knowledge used in work, sharing knowledge throughout the organization,

> An intervention that might improve a customer service rep's productivity is unlikely to fit the job of a scientist.

and injecting knowledge into key processes. Many companies built these repositories, but in general they weren't very successful. Particularly in today's tough economy, most knowledge workers just don't have the time to access and sort through repositories that often contain large quantities of documents of variable quality.

Technology still has an important role to play in knowledge work, but it needs to be integrated with and embedded into day-to-day activities. The approaches that do work seem inconsistent with the move to global, virtual organizations. When we asked managers of successful knowledge work processes at DaimlerChrysler what they'd done to achieve their results, they mentioned rudimentary techniques like putting all workers needed to design a car into the same part of the building. Toyota spoke of using a "big open room" to get all the functions needed to build a car talking with one another. Exxon Mobil described a team-based, parallel approach to bidding on oil exploration leases, in which geologists, engineers, and business planners worked together in one room, rather than the old individual, sequential approach.

These managers occasionally mentioned simple tools such as e-mail and databases as productivity aids, but never any exotic technologies.

What also became clear in subsequent research was that it's impossible to improve the productivity of all knowledge workers in the same way within an organization. An intervention to improve productivity that might work for a customer service rep in a call center is unlikely to fit the job of a research scientist. Furthermore, all types of knowledge work jobs are not of equal importance to organizations.

Therefore, managers wishing to enhance productivity need to segment their knowledge workers. They need to identify the different types of knowledge work that take place in their organizations and the kinds of interventions that are most likely to make sense. They also need to identify the knowledge work jobs that are truly "mission critical"—those roles in which increased productivity is essential to the strategy.

Figure 1 shows one such segmentation scheme (see "A Segmentation Scheme for Knowledge Work"). In that model, individually organized academic scientists or small-practice attorneys might fit into the "expert workers" category, while call center representatives and retail salespeople could be categorized as "transaction workers." In more collaborative processes, automobile design engineers would be "integrated workers," and strategic

FIGURE-1

A segmentation scheme for knowledge work

Integrated Workers	**Collaborative Workers**	
• Systematic, repeatable work	• Improvisational work	
• Relies on formal processes, methodologies, or standards	• Highly reliant on deep expertise across multiple functions	
• Needs tight integration across functional boundaries	• Involves flexible teams deployed fluidly	
Transaction Workers	**Expert Workers**	
• Routine work	• Judgment-oriented work	
• Relies on formal rules, procedures, and training	• Relies on individual expertise and experience	
• Employs low-discretion workforce or automation	• Employs star performers	

Collaborative groups — Individual actors (Level of Interdependence)

Routine ← Complexity of work → Interpretation/judgment

planners or investment bankers "collaborative workers." Diversified firms might have all four types, or even more, based on other dimensions.

The key to improving productivity is to tailor the intervention to the type of work. For transaction workers, it's common to "script" the work using databases and workflow automation tools. A call center rep is often told what to say under every circumstance and in response to every imaginable customer comment or question. Access to knowledge resources is tightly constrained by the need for heads-down productivity and responsiveness to customers; there isn't the time to search through a repository.

Such a solution would hardly apply to collaborative workers, whose job processes involve too much uncertainty to be scripted. These workers are best served by a series of tools they can draw upon as needed; the individual worker remains the integrator of the tools and knowledge.

Integrated workers need templates and job aids that make it easy to reuse existing intellectual assets, such as engineering designs for components. Major automobile companies such as GM and Ford have found that engineers can't be forced to use these assets, but will do so if it's the path of least resistance.

Interventions for expert workers may be the most difficult to attempt. Such workers have historically had a great deal of autonomy and their jobs have had little structure. They also care a great deal about the quality of their work, so improved quality must be an attribute of any improvement effort.

There have been some successes in this category, however. Partners HealthCare System, which consists of several Harvard-affiliated teaching hospitals, implemented a physician order-entry system that adds intelligence to the patient-care process while preserving the ability of physicians to overrule the system's recommendations for medications, tests, or referrals. The system has reduced adverse drug events by 55%, lowering costs for medical errors while improving physician productivity and patient care. Partners focused its efforts on the most important knowledge work role in patient care: the physician.

For too long, knowledge work has been ignored by organizations seeking to enhance productivity. This group is too large and too important to the success of today's firms to bypass. By segmenting and targeting particular types of knowledge workers, we can begin to achieve a revolution of postindustrial work.

Reprint U0211E

Intellectual Capital for the Perplexed

• • •

Mattison Crowe

Think of it as a key concept, maybe even a paradigm, that has just begun to jell. Intellectual capital has provoked a lot of talk of late, and promises to become even more important (conventional wisdom holds it out as the single most valuable corporate asset in the 21st century). But it still remains a bit soft around the edges. What follows is an attempt, in unintimidating question-and-answer format, to summarize the basics.

What is intellectual capital?

Larry Prusak of Ernst & Young defines it as "intellectual material that has been formalized, captured, and leveraged to produce a higher value asset." A contemporary example is Netscape's capacity to take a programmer's concept and transform it into thousands of lines of code that are developed, tested, modified, and eventually released as a Web browser. Intellectual capital includes more than just the end product: It comprises all the learning, and infrastructure, that allow its possessor to get the product onto the market, achieve a better result than competing firms, and repeat the process more rapidly the next time round.

The use of our human intelligence has been described as transforming "knowings" along the following lines:

data→information→
knowledge→wisdom

Similarly, the development of intellectual capital can be compared to a manufacturing process, in which raw materials are converted into finished products. Managing intellectual capital involves selecting information from various locations and moving it along a chain in which value is added until it attains its highest worth. This capability will become increasingly important. As Peter Drucker reminds us, "Knowledge is power, which is why people who had it in the past often tried to make a secret of it. In post-capitalism, power comes from transmitting information to make it productive, not from hiding it."

How much is an organization's intellectual capital typically worth?

A huge question. You will know that the paradigm has jelled when consensus arrives at a generally accepted or standard measure of the value of a company's intellectual capital. Up until now, traditional financial reporting has largely failed to engage the question. As a result, we're left with guesses. Charles Handy estimates the value at three to four times the book value of a company's tangible assets; other estimates spiral upward from there.

As I begin to look at my own company's intellectual capital, and to think about building it, what should I keep in mind?

Your company's business strategy. Why bother to look for something if you are uncertain how it will help you? From the beginning, make sure that your efforts are framed with an eye toward understanding how better knowledge will improve your business. In an article in

Fast Company, McKinsey consultants Brook Manville and Nathaniel Foote argue that a "company has to know the kind of value it intends to provide and to whom. Only then can it link its knowledge resources in a way that makes a difference: serving customers around the world in a coordinated, consistent manner; responding quickly and efficiently to changing competitive conditions; offering its products or services to customers more quickly, cheaply, efficiently and innovatively."

What tools do I have at my disposal for tracking this elusive commodity?

As on any frontier, most of the primitive road maps for charting intellectual capital are unreliable. Leif Edvinsson, vice president and director of intellectual capital for Skandia Assurance and Financial Services, and Michael Malone have developed a reporting model that tracks up to 35 indices in five broad categories—financial, customer, process, renewal and development, and human. Their measures range from the straightforward (market share) to the dubious (an empowerment index?). Malone and Edvinsson hope to win acceptance for their reporting scheme and eventually to see a document that incorporates it included as a supplement to a company's annual report.

For all such efforts, though, it quickly becomes apparent to any student of the subject that new methods for quantifying such a slippery asset remain incomplete. Even Edvinsson and Malone's scheme, while appearing exhaustive in the scope of its reporting, doesn't necessarily indicate which factors are most critical. But can you afford to wait for Generally Accepted Accounting Principles on intellectual capital to appear? Probably not.

So where to begin digging? You might start by considering intellectual capital to consist of three components: human capital, structural capital, and customer capital. While each will be described at greater length below, keep in mind that these three don't function, or in some sense even exist, in isolation from one another; value is created only as a result of their interplay.

What is human capital?

As the old saw would have it, those assets that go home at 5 p.m. Except that at, say, a hot software firm, they may stay all night. The new reality is that for a business to compete successfully in the new millennium, it's probably going to need better access to its potential brainpower. In order to map out what kinds of human capital you want to exploit and nurture, you have to begin with—what else?—strategy. Cast a critical eye at your work force, and look at what types of skills it contributes to your business.

Tom Stewart, author of *Intellectual Capital: The New Wealth of Organizations,* proposes that you focus resources on those employees with "proprietary skills." Proprietary skills are the unique talents an employee possesses around which a company builds a business. IDEO is the premier industrial-product design firm by virtue of the talents of its designers; they enable the firm to command a premium over the offerings of its competitors. This is where competitive advantage is created and sustained. The bulk of your organization's resources should be used to benefit the efforts of your key people. An informal test is to ask yourself, "If _____ resigned tomorrow, how easily could we replace her and what would be the impact on our organization?"

What is structural capital?

If you envision your company as a person, and human capital represents the mind of that person, structural capital would represent the body—the part that allows the ideas to manifest themselves. In this emerging paradigm, its raison d'être is to give context to human and customer capital, amplify them through the organization, and capture knowledge so it can be "owned" by shareholders over time. Examples of structural capital include:

- databases, reports, manuals

- information systems (intranets and groupware being the sexiest of this lot)

- intellectual property that is afforded legal protection (patents, copyrights, trademarks, trade secrets, etc.)

- organizational goals and the strategy behind them

- formal hierarchy in terms of individual responsibilities and accountability

- the collective beliefs, opinions, history, myths, values, and mindset that govern people's "way" of doing things; in other words, the culture

For most organizations, structural capital needs to evolve through a process described as "knowledge conversion" by Ikujiro Nonaka and Hirotaka Takeuchi in *The Knowledge Creating Company*. Knowledge conversion means translating tacit knowledge into explicit knowledge (so it can be examined) and back to tacit knowledge again (for rapid implementation). Allowing intellectual capital to move through this cycle ensures that knowledge is congruent, captured, and leveraged to give it the highest value.

What is customer capital?

So now we have mind and body. What's left? Customer capital represents the environment in which this mind/

body system operates. It refers to the organization's relationships or networks. Of the three elements that make up intellectual capital, it's the one that people most often have a tough time understanding. Think of it as comprising

- customers

- suppliers

- market channels

- industry associations and trade groups

- government policymakers

Customer capital embodies all the data, opinions, and values collectively held about your business by these groups. Market share, customer retention, and per-customer profitability are all measures designed to gauge how well a company is doing in managing this kind of capital.

One of the more interesting observations from the intellectual-capital folks is that over time, knowledge becomes embedded in a market. (Think about how much more customers know today about, say, personal computers compared to the days of the first Apples or Kaypros.) As the quantity of such knowledge grows, the tendency is for it to flow more quickly toward the customer. This is only one more reminder that customers have the ultimate say in the success of a business, and nowadays they are better informed about their choices than ever before. Customer-capital experts also note that the more mature the market, the more tacit the embedded knowledge becomes. To make sense of it all, your company will require more frequent and intensive contact with the market.

What are the most useful tools to measure, capture, and exploit intellectual capital?

We'll describe five. Bear in mind that the goal of each is to develop networks of people who collaborate, not networks of technology that interconnect. And unless they are of demonstrable value in helping to serve customers, people won't use them.

Competency Maps

Employees consult these to understand what skills and attributes they will need if they are to do their current jobs successfully and to further develop professionally. Devised as an alternative to traditional training, their use was pioneered by Hubert Saint-Onge, vice president of learning organization and leadership development at the Canadian Imperial Bank of Commerce. Employees there were given descriptions of competencies derived from surveys that asked customers about their expectations. By acquiring or augmenting these competencies, they could move further along their desired career path.

CIBC subsequently abolished formal training. Instead, managers were told to let employees shadow their more expert colleagues for periods of time. Every branch was provided with a "learning room" where employees could take out books and software. People could also sign up for courses if they wished. The key difference from the traditional training scheme is the new system relies on the individual's aspirations; the result is a knowledge pull, not an information push, so learning occurs just in time, right when that person needs it most, for the greatest impact.

Communities of Practice

In the past, you might not have had a formal name for groups like these; they were just people who met twice a month for a brown bag lunch to discuss issues that had to do with your order processing system, for instance. Alternatively dubbed "worknets," communities of practice are described by Brook Manville as "a group of professionals, informally bound to one another through exposure to a common class of problems, common pursuit of solutions, and thereby themselves embodying a store of knowledge."

The warmest and fuzziest of the ways to build human capital, communities of practice can, when executed correctly, create knowledge as well as transfer it. Membership should range across departmental, functional, and even organizational boundaries. Participants take the lessons developed within the group and spread the knowledge unobtrusively. While such groups may form spontaneously and not require much in the way of formal company resources, you must encourage their efforts and resist the temptation to formally manage their activity or to expect a deliverable in turn. High-value workers appreciate being offered the latitude to interact this way and may become less likely to tote their brainpower somewhere else.

Corporate Yellow Pages

Leif Edvinsson laments, "Technologies such as e-mail and the Internet facilitate the rapid exchange of knowledge, but they do not help identify the relevant knowledge or who has it." One way to combat this problem is to organize an index of experts within the organization by field of inquiry. Transforming the ad hoc tedium of locating an authority into a high-velocity process helps the company accumulate human capital as a "stock" and avoids duplicative, wasteful searching for information.

Lessons Database

Few companies have developed an immunity to the problem of "losing the recipe." Almost every project, regardless of its outcome, has some transferable lessons that could benefit others within the organization. A data warehouse of key lessons archived for future reference shows how tacit knowledge can be converted into explicit files which then become available to everyone. Consult your information technology experts to see if they can develop a system to classify groups of solutions that worked—and those that failed—by subject or type of project. The solution may be as simple as an off-the-shelf database or groupware program. You might reinforce this with a stipulation that every project or sale has an entry in the database as part of a formal debriefing process.

Knowledge Forum

While corporate Yellow Pages and lessons databases represent the concept of a knowledge "stock," the forum is more akin to a knowledge "flow." It offers a virtual space where all an organization's human and customer capital can interact. At Buckman Laboratories International, a specialty chemicals manufacturer, creating such a system entailed putting the company's communications network up on Compuserve, which allowed the creation of private bulletin boards for intrafirm usage. Any employee of the company could connect with another in one phone call, and also link to headquarters from anywhere in the world.

Used in concert with communities of practice, such forums obliterate many of the time and geographical barriers to collaboration. You can also bring customers and suppliers aboard, sometimes in the process gaining valuable intelligence on your competitors. The more participants you open this forum to, the more robust it becomes. But that, in general, is the way it is with intellectual capital.

For Further Reading

"Developing a Model for Intellectual Capital" by Leif Edvinsson and Patrick Sullivan (*European Management Journal*, Vol. 14 No. 4, August 1996)

"Strategy As If Knowledge Mattered" by Brook Manville and Nathaniel Foote (*Fast Company*, April/May 1996)

"New Metrics for a New Age" by Michael S. Malone (*Forbes ASAP*, April 7, 1997)

Intellectual Capital: The New Wealth of Organizations by Thomas A. Stewart (1996, Doubleday/Currency)

The Knowledge Creating Company: How Japanese Companies Create the Dynamics of Innovation by Ikujiro Nonaka and Hirotaka Takeuchi (1995, Oxford University Press)

"Buckman Labs Is Nothing but Net" by Glenn Rifkin (*Fast Company*, June/July 1996)

"Tacit Knowledge: The key to the strategic alignment of intellectual capital" by Hubert Saint-Onge (*Strategy and Leadership*, March/April 1996, Vol. 24 No. 2)

Reprint U9708C

When Your Best People Leave, Will Their Knowledge Leave, Too?

• • •

David Boath and David Y. Smith

Executives often speak of their most important resource as the one that walks out the door each night. Yet few leaders are sufficiently guarding their organizations against the day when key people walk out the door for good. And with the rebounding economy, that day may be coming sooner than many firms would like to admit. More so, as the workforce ages—and workers of all ages continue to be more transient—many companies are looking at an ongoing, irreplaceable loss of the knowledge, experience, and wisdom that have been a primary source of competitiveness and profitability.

> ## Don't lose the great body of knowledge represented by your workforce.

That is, unless they begin to execute a strategic plan of action to retain and build on the great body of knowledge represented by their workforce. Such a plan should have the following goals:

- Help people capture and distribute knowledge— both their own and that of their coworkers.

- Support collaboration across time and space.

- Provide access to the learning and performance support needed to work most effectively.

- Implement organizational structures that lead to effective career development and succession planning.

The loss of knowledge and its effects on workforce productivity and performance represent a complex web of issues. It stands to reason, then, that no single or monolithic solution can address all the issues. Instead, organizations need to think in terms of a suite of strategies, techniques, and technologies. Companies seeking to pursue such an approach should follow these steps:

Identify the knowledge most at risk and institutionalize it

Companies should begin by identifying where they are most at risk from the loss of information and experience. This involves, in part, establishing performance-management and career-development processes that carry with them the identification of employees who possess the most critical knowledge.

For example, as David W. De Long and Thomas O. Mann noted in "Stemming the Brain Drain" in *Outlook Journal*, "When air traffic dropped dramatically after September 11," Delta Air Lines cut the workforce to remain competitive. "So when 11,000 employees company-wide agreed to take an early retirement or severance offer, Delta had less than two months to identify those employees who held jobs for which no backups or replacements had been trained . . . and then capture that knowledge before it walked out the door. Supervisors across the board worked with a team from Delta's learning services unit to narrow the list of 11,000 down to those veterans whose departure would represent a 'critical job loss.' Once these outstanding performers were identified, they were interviewed about their roles at the company. This way, Delta retained as much critical knowledge as possible on very short notice."

Establish more focused career-development and succession-planning programs

A career-development program builds knowledge that professionals need to prepare for future roles. For example, following a recent fourfold increase in new-drug discoveries, Wyeth recognized that its 150 clinical study team leaders had become a mission-critical workforce among its 6,000 employees in research and development.

In an effort to retain and develop these increasingly important managers, the company developed a unique career-progression model that defined a set of critical competencies—as well as the required levels of proficiency—for each career level. It assessed all clinical study team leaders against those competencies and created individual development plans to address opportunities for improvement and growth. Wyeth also built tools to enhance clinical study team leaders' knowledge further and established collaboration forums to allow continued learning and sharing of best practices.

Additionally, to help ensure that the organization's

expertise in trial management continues to grow, clinical study team leaders join so-called capability teams, where they address process changes and training needs, and they are also now part of a new, centralized organization focused specifically on trial management.

Build knowledge communities

In many organizations, knowledge resides solely with "experts," who take their knowledge with them when they leave. The right collaboration tools can capture experts' information and insights and help build a community around them, transforming their knowledge into community knowledge. One of the more seamless ways this can happen is by saving and archiving instant messaging (IM) conversations involving key company experts. Often filled with insight, these conversations are

> Organizational knowledge loss is a systemic problem involving the entire employment life cycle.

Combating "Brain Drain"

Organizational knowledge loss is a systemic problem involving the entire employment life cycle: recruiting, hiring, performance, retention, and retirement. Companies may be tempted to implement a number of nonintegrated solutions. While some of these—such as mentoring programs, knowledge databases, or hiring retirees as contractors—have some value, most are merely quick fixes, and comprehensive problems need comprehensive and integrated solutions.

Firms should implement the following to ensure they retain the expertise required to stay competitive:

- Workforce planning and organizational design, which ensures that structures and processes are in place to support career development, identification of most vital personnel, and succession planning.

- Workforce support and collaboration, using portal and enterprise resource management solutions.

- Learning design and delivery, focusing on anytime, anywhere learning and the powerful solutions found in today's performance simulation solutions.

generally lost as soon as they disappear from computer screens. But new tools capture them and make them available for retrieval, thus ensuring that the knowledge transmitted through them remains in-house.

Adopt more advanced e-learning techniques, especially performance simulation

E-learning has revolutionized workforce training. Freeing organizations from a restrictive belief that learning happens only when it's "officially" administered in classroom settings, e-learning has permitted a consistent distribution of high-quality content, enabling anytime, anywhere learning that is learner-driven.

Performance simulations, in particular, have proven to be highly effective learning techniques. Completing tasks in an environment that looks like the real thing—with rules-based feedback and remediation—provides insights, assessments, and coaching. Learners are directed to expert "war stories" and perspectives, specific reference materials, industry best practices, and practice activities, which they learn and apply to complete the task successfully. All of the material is available to learners at precisely the moments they are primed to learn—at the points of trial and error.

For example, to boost profitability and respond to change more quickly, Siemens' global workforce had to learn to speak a common financial language. The company used a 48-hour simulation experience designed for 10,000 finance and business professionals. With a combination of technology and group-based activities, they simulated the challenge of growing a single-product

65

company focused on the domestic market into a global industrial organization facing complex business decisions. The exercises allowed participants to practice the roles of financial analyst, finance manager, and project controller. In business review meetings, they worked in teams to complete a case study, drawing on expertise gained in previous simulation activities. The result: staff came away from the simulation with both a more deeply engrained understanding of the pressing need for a common language and a more robust grip on the language itself.

Reprint U0409C

Managing Knowledge in Your Team

. . .

How might you best manage knowledge in your team, department, or division? The articles in this section provide potent tips and tools—including ways to encourage employees to share what they know, choose a knowledge management process, gather intelligence about competitors, and ensure that the knowledge workers on your team get the support and resources they need to produce value for your organization.

Knowledge Management

Four Practical Steps

• • •

Diane McFerrin Peters

Most companies underestimate the importance of intangible assets such as knowledge, creativity, ideas, and relationships. All these account for more value in our economy than the tangibles. Yet it's difficult for companies to get their arms around intangibles, so they rarely protect them as carefully as they do bricks and hardware. What would you do if your smartest people suddenly left? How can you ensure that what one department or division learns is widely shared throughout the company?

The discipline of knowledge management (KM) was designed to answer questions such as these. In many companies, however, KM is limited to patents and other issues related to the ownership of ideas. If you really want to develop and utilize your intangibles, KM must mean something else: it must enable your company to cultivate and share new ideas, and it must focus your company's brainpower on what's really important. You don't have to be CEO to implement KM of this sort; the elements can be applied in any department, division, or location. To get started, I recommend four practical steps:

Create a Setting for Sharing Knowledge

Access to knowledge breeds more knowledge, and the best KM techniques ensure that everyone's involved. Rosenbluth International, a travel services firm where I was chief communications officer, has an open meeting policy. With few exceptions, everyone can attend any meeting. Meetings are announced daily to make it easy, resulting in faster sharing and cross-cultivation of knowledge and ideas. At Hewitt Associates, an HR consulting firm, KM is practiced in ways both symbolic and real. Conference rooms all have round tables, so no one can sit at the head and dictate discussions. Nobody has a corner office, and there are no titles. Everyone has access to Lotus Notes databases, and associates share what they know across practice, office, and geographic boundaries.

Eliminate Communication "Filters"

Politics, turf, and implementation responsibilities can squelch ideas in traditional communication channels. Going outside the channels—for example, by allowing people to skip levels—leads to more ideas on how to do things better. Alagasco, a natural gas company, provides a direct link to CEO Mike Warren via cards posted throughout the organization. Employees jot down questions and ideas, with no signature required. Rosenbluth has a toll-free hotline to CEO Hal Rosenbluth. Insurance and financial-services giant USAA has an online system enabling employees to share opinions and ideas spontaneously and anonymously.

Prioritize the Tasks

Most companies' to-do lists contain twice as much as they could ever accomplish. A prioritization process can align brainpower and effort behind what's truly strategic. Senior leaders get together to rank all vital activities first to last, no ties allowed. The process lets people challenge assumptions about the value of long-running projects, share knowledge about what is being accomplished, and break down the departmental barriers that bottle up ideas and creativity. If something is ranked priority one, everyone must contribute to its success.

Keep Time Budgets

Few individuals and fewer organizations get a true read on where their time and effort really go. Try having each person keep a log of their activities in 15-minute increments for a few days. Leaders then submit "time budgets" of exactly how time is being spent in their areas. Seeing the aggregate results for your entire organization can be an eye-opener. You'll find some things you want to put an end to and others that can be streamlined. Most important, you'll see whether day-to-day activity reflects your strategic priorities. Effective KM requires people to spend time developing, applying, and sharing ideas. You can see from the time budgets whether they're really doing it.

Picasso had a collection of masterpieces in his home. They were hung slightly crooked, and visitors couldn't resist the temptation to straighten them. But Picasso felt that when a painting was straight, the observer focused on the frame around it. When the frame was crooked, the beauty of the image jumped out. It's the same with knowledge. Instead of trying to put boundaries around it, we should be letting it jump out of its frame.

Reprint U0003D

Managing Knowledge

How to Make Money with What You Know

• • •

Rebecca M. Saunders

Every day, knowledge essential to your business walks out your door, and much of it never comes back. Employees leave, customers come and go—and their knowledge leaves with them. This information drain costs you time, money, and customers.

You need a knowledge management (KM) program. When done right, it helps you understand your customers better, bring products to market faster, or run your plants more smoothly.

Of course, this is hardly news. Yet few companies have created successful KM programs. They're hard to get started—and harder still to make work.

So what do you need to put together a successful program? We went to companies that have made great progress in KM for some advice.

Define Your Program's Value Proposition

You need to be explicit about what you want to achieve as a result of your KM program. Most KM efforts are driven by one of three objectives: increased customer intimacy, faster time to market, or operational excellence. In the high-tech industry, for example, time to market is often the key difference between suppliers, so that would be the main focus of a KM program. A company that doesn't roll out too many new products, on the other hand—like Chevron—will focus its KM efforts on operational excellence.

Choose a Process

Most KM efforts fall into one of three categories:

Self-directed

The company provides the database technology, and employees use it to find the information they need.

Tools may include a pointer system directing the user to an expert or even a search engine. These databases depend on user initiative. They are a good, low-cost system for capturing the explicit knowledge of the organization, but they can't capture the tacit knowledge in employees' heads.

Knowledge Networks

Consulting companies in particular have experimented widely with knowledge networks. Index Consulting, for example, the firm that championed re-engineering, tried to capture the knowledge learned on various re-engineering projects in order to make it easier to tackle the next project that came along. Typically, the companies find (as Index did) that employees are happy to use the networks for information, but less excited about putting in the enormous amounts of time required in keeping them up to date.

Facilitated Transfer

This is the full-service approach. In addition to the previous components, it designates specific individuals who spend either part or all of their time integrating best practices or encouraging knowledge transfer throughout the organization. Facilitators assist with implementation by linking best practices to business problems. They also show others how to participate in knowledge sharing and transfer. Companies using this

Using Learning Histories

Companies possess two types of knowledge. The first is explicit or external: it consists of what is known about processes and procedures, and may include books, white papers, policy and procedural manuals, and databases. Technology tools are great for organizing and providing open access to this important knowledge. The other type of knowledge is harder to codify: it's the knowledge that resides in the heads of all the people in the organization, its customers, and its suppliers. Part of the institutional memory, it is referred to as "tacit knowledge" by organizational learning expert Ikujiro Nonaka, now Xerox Distinguished Professor of Knowledge at the University of California at Berkeley Haas School of Business.

Arthur Kleiner, coauthor (with George Roth) of *Car Launch: The Human Side of Managing Change,* focuses on learning histories, or storytelling that helps codify the tacit knowledge of an organization that would otherwise get lost. Kleiner describes the learning history technique as a way to "jump start teams" and "help senior executives who don't get knowledge coming from below." They have formalized the technique of storytelling by gathering people in study groups to tell their own stories about projects that have been both successes and failures. "The greatest benefit of a learning history is that it makes an organization get serious about learning mechanisms to codify and come to terms with their collective experience and develop their organizational memory."

fully dedicated approach include Texas Instruments, Amoco, and Raytheon.

Find and Enlist the Right People

Facilitators usually come from inside the organization: they may be internal consultants, change agents, team leaders, or benchmarking coordinators. Bill Baker, Raytheon's "benchmarking/knowledge transfer champion," says Raytheon asked its managers to identify the people who should be involved in the process. To keep balance in the recruiting process, the company recruited individuals from every discipline and geographical location.

Make Sure the Technology Supports Your Data

There are plenty of software programs to facilitate the IT part of the knowledge management equation. Raytheon wanted a program that would be useful to a broad cross-section of people, says Baker, so it decided on a Lotus Notes application. Team members from all over the company act as knowledge editors in the system, adding key words and reworking the material to make it more searchable. The Lotus Notes Knowledgebase is accessible via Raytheon's intranet. Employees can search through a benchmarking library and the best practice Knowledge-base as well as submit best practices.

Invest in Training Knowledge Workers

Data-capturing and data-sharing technologies are important, but they're only part of the story. Employees need a system for getting information to flow. For instance, newspapers provide information management skills to their reporters so they're not constantly reinventing the wheel with every story. "Newspeople traffic in information every day, producing knowledge products on time, on deadline, and without missing a beat. It's a team effort," says Amy Zuckerman, a consultant and author. Employees need to be trained to practice KM in the same way. In the corporate world, according to Zuckerman, "the investment in technology is there, but often the people skills are shortchanged, because management thinks that knowledge management is all about the technology." Raytheon's Baker agrees: "Facilitators need special skills. Training is necessary to capture and disseminate knowledge."

Employees need to learn how to map and articulate processes as well as how best to question others when asking about their best practices. For instance, asking "why" is often an inappropriate way to learn more since it can put those being questioned on the defensive.

Focus on Your Strategy

At Chevron, the central theme of the corporate KM strategy is "connections." Jeff Stemke, an internal consultant, refers to himself as "an evangelist for KM." The practice focuses on four variations on the connections theme. "We connect people to the explicit knowledge we have—for example, on the intranet, using tools similar to a Yahoo-like map or portal searching tools. We connect people to others who can help them answer questions or solve problems with a yellow pages/expertise locator. We connect people to communities of practice to share what they know, to learn from each other, and to develop new knowledge. This takes what we've done with best practice teams over the last few years and makes it more of a day-to-day activity. Finally, we look for ways to connect our knowledge and people into our processes, products, and services."

Some more advice:

Get Buy-in from Senior Management

Knowledge management requires a long-term effort. This means, says Baker, "you need commitment—believers at the senior management level." If you don't have management buy-in, "you won't have the resources, the people, or the tools to get the job done or the cultural change necessary to get people to share their knowledge."

Measuring Results

Assessment is the least developed aspect of knowledge transfer, according to Carla O'Dell and C. Jackson Grayson, Jr., authors of *If Only We Knew What We Know.* There are two camps on the subject of measuring results: the "nurturers" who believe that trying to measure before you understand how knowledge is created and shared may lead you to focus on the wrong things, and the "quantifiers" who believe measurement is important for "determining where and how to invest." Chevron falls into the latter category: it has been developing and sharing best practices since the early 1990s and shows improvement on several metrics. Chevron's Jeff Stemke points to a $2 billion a year savings in operating costs—not wholly attributable to KM, he says, "but development of best practices was an important area. We have saved over $1 billion in the last seven years on energy consumption, one of our best practice focus areas, and our safety record shows a drop of over 50% in incidents and injuries." Other companies have less tangible results but feel they have made significant gains in the customer relationship area, according to O'Dell and Grayson.

Focus on Solutions to Key Problems

To ensure long-term success in your knowledge management efforts, Stemke advises focusing on the issues that are most important to your company. "For Chevron, the key driver is how to be cost effective." Early efforts identified the organization's key processes, products, and services and what knowledge was necessary to make them work effectively.

Teach Employees to Share Their Knowledge

Getting people to willingly and openly share is the hardest part of knowledge transfer. Raytheon assigned people to facilitate the sharing, says Baker. "We had to go in and get people to share their know-how."

Think of Knowledge Management as a Race

There are three laps in the knowledge race at Raytheon. The first is capturing knowledge. The second is interpreting what is known. The third is deploying it, says Baker. "The whole race is based on speed. We have to beat the competition in this race."

For Further Reading

Smart Things to Know About Knowledge Management by Thomas Koulopoulos (1999, Capstone Ltd.)

Harvard Business Review on Knowledge Management (1998, Harvard Business School Press)

If Only We Knew What We Know by Carla O'Dell and C. Jackson Grayson, Jr., with Nilly Essaides (1998, Free Press)

Car Launch: The Human Side of Managing Change by George Roth and Art Kleiner (1999, Getty Center for Education in the Arts)

Reprint C0006A

Debriefing Gabriel Szulanski

Improving Best-Practice Transfer

• • •

Lauren Keller Johnson

It all sounds so easy: The people in Unit A of your company are remarkably talented at, say, product design—and you want to duplicate their talent in Units B, C, and D. But when you try to transfer this best practice, the effort falls flat. Employees in Unit B prove unable to apply the practice. Those in Unit C balk at adopting it. And although workers in Unit D gamely implement the practice, the business results pale next to those of Unit A. Frustrated, you abandon the effort.

If it's any comfort, you're not alone. According to Gabriel Szulanski, author of *Sticky Knowledge: Barriers to*

Knowing in the Firm and associate professor of strategy and management at INSEAD, most firms encounter huge difficulties in trying to spread best practices. And this is despite the abundance of "stellar performance in their own backyards." Unable to leverage existing knowledge, firms end up with performance gaps of 200% or more between comparable units—gaps worth millions.

How can executives make their companies' existing knowledge less "sticky" and capture the financial gains awaiting them if they can close those performance gaps? Szulanski says firms must recognize that there are unique challenges present in managing the transfer of internal knowledge, and so managers must look beyond familiar motivational factors—e.g., "source" employees' unwillingness to share data for fear of losing their jobs, or "recipient" employees' resistance to change. Managers, he says, must also attend to these seven *knowledge barriers*, which he breaks into four categories:

Knowledge characteristics

1. CAUSAL AMBIGUITY: We can't know with full certainty what's causing exceptional performance and how those forces might interact in another unit.

2. UNPROVEN KNOWLEDGE: When trying to transfer a recently developed best practice, we can't trust that knowledge to be effective in a new situation.

Source characteristics

3. LACK OF CREDIBILITY: High-performing unit members aren't perceived as knowledgeable or trustworthy by others in the organization.

Recipient characteristics

4. LACK OF ABSORPTIVE CAPACITY: People don't recognize the value of new knowledge. Moreover, they lack the skills, shared language, and experience to put new knowledge to work.

5. LACK OF RETENTIVE CAPACITY: People don't use transferred knowledge enough to embed it in the way they do their work.

Cultural characteristics

6. "BARRENNESS": The company lacks systems and structures to enable people to recognize and seize opportunities to leverage existing knowledge.

7. LACK OF "INTIMATE" RELATIONSHIPS BETWEEN SOURCES AND RECIPIENTS: People from different units don't have a history of positive communication and collaboration.

"Unsticking" Knowledge

According to Szulanski's research, the three most daunting knowledge barriers are causal ambiguity, recipient employees' lack of absorptive capacity, and lack of intimate relationships between sources and recipients. Though we can't clear up causal ambiguity entirely, Szulanski says we *can* dig more deeply to discover why a successful practice works so well. "In companies where exemplary processes have been in place for 20 years," he says, "you need to ask people *why* they do what they do—and *how*. Consider your depth of knowledge of the practice, then ask yourself, 'What's the potential gain of applying this practice in another unit? How long will it take to start getting equal or better results in the recipient unit?' All knowledge barriers take time to remove, so you have to make a tradeoff."

Surmounting the absorptive-capacity barrier seems more straightforward. Indeed, Szulanski has seen many companies make a concerted effort to address this "stickiness predictor." Key strategies include investing in training and education to ensure that members of a recipient unit have the skills, along with the technical and managerial competence, to absorb the new practice. In addition, managers need to communicate the vision of what the company is trying to achieve through the transfer of existing knowledge. Finally, to improve their absorptive capacity, recipients must possess the vocabulary to talk about the transferred practice and must clearly define the roles and responsibilities essential for implementing the practice. If training and education don't yield results, Szulanski says, "managers should hire new people who *can* absorb the transferred practice."

As for the lack of intimate relationships between sources and recipients, Szulanski recommends doing whatever it takes to forge bonds between people. "In intimate relationships," he says, "people feel invested in those bonds. They enjoy interacting, they collaborate quickly and more productively, and they're more responsive to each other. All this is essential in best-practice transfer—because the two parties must interact repeatedly over long periods of time."

To foster close relationships, you can relax limits on travel and communication, and look for chances to promote teamwork between affected groups. "When Hewlett-Packard needed to transfer design practices from the U.S. to Singapore," Szulanski says, "it gave the two groups of engineers opportunities to spend time together under some fairly adverse circumstances. They went on treks [in] the Rocky Mountains—but the most powerful relationship-building experience they had involved eating Mexican food together. When you and your soon-to-be teammates are suffering from hot peppers, you bond pretty quickly!"

The Importance of Timing

Szulanski also advises managers to distinguish among four stages of best-practice transfer:

1. INITIATION: Recognizing and acting on an opportunity to transfer knowledge.

2. IMPLEMENTATION: Exchanging information and resources between source and recipient.

3. RAMP-UP: Beginning to use the transferred knowledge and rectifying unexpected problems.

4. INTEGRATION: Making the transferred practice routine.

"Different knowledge barriers become more of a problem at different stages," Szulanski says. For example, "Source credibility, provenness of knowledge, and causal ambiguity are particularly important during the initiation stage, whereas absorptive capacity becomes more of an issue during implementation, ramp-up, and integration." Equally important, "The sooner you start addressing knowledge barriers, the better—because they all take time to remove. If you wait too long to deal with them, you may already be up to your neck in costly mistakes."

Szulanski's study also explored the impact of motivational barriers at each of the four transfer stages. His findings revealed some surprising complexities. Specifically, it turns out that a recipient who's highly motivated to implement a best practice from another unit can actually *intensify* transfer problems during the ramp-up stage. Why? The person may prematurely dismiss outside help, expand seemingly straightforward modifications into major projects, make unnecessary changes to preserve pride of ownership and status, or switch to new practices at the worst possible moment because of unchecked enthusiasm. Recipients' motivation, Szulanski writes, "may therefore be helpful for initiating a transfer but may complicate its implementation."

To Copy or Not to Copy?

Szulanski's findings suggests several significant implications for managers. For one thing, "Managing for use of existing knowledge is different from managing to create *new* knowledge," he states. "In the first case, you want people to copy what's working well, get results, and only then start tinkering with the process to fix problems. In the second case, you'd probably want to *prohibit* copying. These are contradictory principles, so you have to be clear about when you're doing which."

In the face of causal ambiguity, "we must also accept that we don't know what we're doing—even while needing to act to keep our companies competitive. We have to be both humble and realistic—yet most of us have more confidence than we should in our ability to transfer knowledge." This makes copying even more important. As Szulanski explains, "If early on you start modifying a best practice you're trying to transfer, and then the effort fails in the new situation, you'll be even less able to determine *why* it failed. Your best hope of figuring out the cause of problems is to reproduce the source practice, then compare its new incarnation to the original. In a sense, you're trying to design as controlled an experiment as possible."

Last, Szulanski recommends identifying "a working example of the entire thing you want to copy. Don't cobble together 'the best of the best' or pieces of practices from different sources. A complete working example gives you your best shot at addressing most of the knowledge barriers. You see how the parts connect and interact, so right there, you're reducing causal ambiguity."

Szulanski's study suggests that obstacles to best-practice transfer are far more nuanced and complex than many of us realize. But by understanding the impact of knowledge as well as motivational barriers, we can improve our chances of transplanting exemplary performance across our organizations and better manage our companies' most precious source of competitive advantage.

Reprint U0403E

The Power of Competitive Intelligence

• • •

David Stauffer

A few years ago, in an intelligence coup that rivals any engineered by James Bond, pharmaceutical giant Merck & Co. found clues to the product positioning and marketing strategy that a rival firm was likely to employ when it rolled out a potential major new drug. Merck countered the competitor's anticipated effort by repositioning one of its existing drugs to occupy the competitive space where the rival's drug was likely to be aimed. Merck's intelligence proved spot on. By repositioning its drug, Merck grabbed new market share and forced the competitor back to the drawing board, delaying the competitor's drug's launch by well over a year. Merck figures the cumulative incremental sales value of this single intelligence windfall at more than $300 million.

What masterful spycraft did Merck use to uncover its rival's plans? The answer would hardly qualify as grist for the mill of movie scriptwriters. According to Clifford Kalb, Merck's senior director of strategic business analysis, the firm's people learned much of what they needed by attending medical meetings and carefully combing public information on clinical trials.

Welcome to the modern practice of competitive intelligence (CI), described by Tim Kindler, director of competitive intelligence for Eastman Kodak Company, as "the process of ethically collecting, analyzing, and disseminating accurate, relevant, specific, timely, forward-looking, and actionable intelligence regarding a particular industry or set of competitors." Collecting information about your competitors isn't about back-alley dumpster diving or sending in agents to pose as customers. It's about gleaning insights from competitors' Web sites and

> Almost everyone in your company is doing CI whether they know it or not.

public filings. It's about chatting with industry peers at trade shows. It's about knowing where to look, what to ask, and what to do with what you discover.

Effective CI builds on the tenets of knowledge management by collecting and then disseminating competitive information throughout the enterprise systematically. Yet despite its great potential, relatively few organizations deploy formal CI practices. Most likely, this is because building and maintaining an effective CI program requires substantial program resources, and one can't prove its value to the bottom line until the practice is up and running. But companies that have done CI well swear by it.

Collecting the Data

Almost "everyone in the firm is doing CI whether they know it or not," says University of Pittsburgh business professor John E. Prescott, executive editor of *Competitive Intelligence Review*. If you leaf through a competitor's annual report, chat with a rival firm's CFO at a reception, or read articles about rivals assembled by an online news clipping service, you're doing CI.

CI professionals report their continuing surprise at how much sensitive information will be revealed by a competitor's employees, board members, and other stakeholders to a total stranger or even to someone who frankly admits affiliation with a rival firm. So it's critical to teach employees in your company who may be in positions to learn this information to ask good questions and be good listeners. Indeed, CI experts say that the hands-down champion CI source, both in the value and ease of gathering information, is the company's own employees. "I'd estimate that 90% of everything we need to know is probably already known by someone in the company," says Steven R. Storms, director of competitive analysis for Weyerhaeuser Company.

Giving Meaning to the Data

Collecting competitor information sounds simple enough, and there is ample evidence of its value. So why have so few companies taken up formal CI efforts? The answer may lie less in the effort it takes to find competitor data than in the effort it takes to make use of it.

Both CI consultants and corporate CI managers stress that their work is not just focused on what competitors are up to—it's about taking that information and evaluating it within the larger competitive environment. This may include economic conditions, customer attitudes, potential regulatory actions, political considerations, and so forth. Many executives may not realize the range of inputs that CI uses, says Anja Kober, who is responsible for the strategic early warning system in the corporate strategy department of Deutsche Telekom. "Some of them think it's all market research," she says. "They're treating it as information—a collection and summary of data—rather than as intelligence which adds analysis and interpretation." That causes problems when executives want recommendations based on numbers because true intelligence "can be difficult or impossible to quantify," Kober says.

"Executives who tend to have a reductionist view of information, wanting to simplify it," are likely to be uncomfortable with CI, says Paul Dishman, associate professor of competitive intelligence and marketing at Brigham Young University's Marriott School of Management. Thus, the burden falls on corporate CI managers to take the lead in showing how competitive data can be put to use.

Connecting the Data to the Bottom Line

To make CI work, you've got to get the information from the employee who has it to the one who needs it. The obstacles begin, especially in organizations where CI is a new concept, with the likelihood that the possessor has no idea that the information could be of use to anyone. "We struggle with that all the time," Weyerhaeuser's Storms says. When he succeeds in delivering a key piece of intelligence, "it's not uncommon to have the recipient say, 'Wow, we've been trying to find out about that for months.'"

It is no small challenge to close the corporate intelligence loop, to get that golden nugget of information from the person who hears it to the person who can use it. And that's where a well-coordinated CI team more than earns its keep. The CI team, along with a company's knowledge management group (if one exists), is at the figurative hub of an organization's information-transferring network—receiving data, analyzing it, and routing it to the right people. For this process of information sharing to be effective, the process and employees' contributions to it must be clearly defined. Employees should be assigned to particular roles, and the process should address these and other questions: Does this data have any potential usefulness? Against what backdrop must it be interpreted? Who in the company can make use of this and how?

A piecemeal approach, on the other hand, is not only likely to fail in delivering consistent corporate value from the data collected, but it also will likely prove ineffective in winning over a management team obsessed with numbers.

Storms illustrates the importance of a coordinated CI practice by describing a casual conversation he had with an employee of Weyerhaeuser's Timberlands Business, who mentioned that a competitor had unexpectedly stopped purchasing wood for its paper mill and would be unable to complete some orders. Storms had heard earlier that one of Weyerhaeuser's paper mills was planning to shut down temporarily because it was light on orders. "It was a simple matter to inform the appropriate business that there were some very unhappy customers of our competitor that needed extra production,"

Storms says. This, he asserts, "is an example of how the CI department can be valuable just by sharing information." In other cases, competitive data will require more analysis to be useful. But under any circumstance, for CI to work, it must "be connected to the organization at many different levels in all the businesses."

How to Organize the Effort

In coordinating a company's CI effort, an early consideration is how to organize. Should CI be centralized in its own unit or have representatives in key departments such as R&D, marketing, and sales? Clues are found in a company's overall culture and structure, which means the best answers won't necessarily be the same for any two companies. Merck's Kalb says that the strategic business analysis unit he heads is an "integrated central department" that reflects the company's "highly centralized" structure. "When there are high levels of resource sharing and common customers and competitors, then the CI processes should be centralized, as at Kodak, Motorola, and Dow," says the University of Pittsburgh's Prescott. "When [these levels] are low, then decentralize, as at IBM, GE, and Fidelity."

Then there's the question of when to outsource CI assignments. While the organization's prevailing practice in outsourcing will suggest a response, important additional considerations apply to CI. If the assignment, for example, is to visit competitors' booths at a trade show or to call competitors to ask about their products or services, people who can say they're employed by someone other than your company might gather more and better information. Consultant Jan Herring says that the badges he wears at conferences list his company, not his client's.

Hired consultant or inside practitioner, today's CI professional "is something like that current TV advertising phrase," says Bill Weber, executive director of the Society of Competitive Intelligence Professionals. "'We don't make the decisions, we make decisions better'—we bring a quality of insight to decision making."

Reprint U0310C

Debriefing Thomas Davenport

Are You Getting the Most from Your Knowledge Workers?

● ● ●

Lauren Keller Johnson

Today, knowledge workers make up 25% to 50% of the workforces of advanced economies, says Thomas Davenport, President's Distinguished Professor of Information Technology and Management at Babson College. Knowledge workers invent your new products and services, design your marketing programs, and create your strategies.

These workers "are the horses that pull the plow of economic progress," he writes in his book *Thinking for a*

Living: How to Get Better Performance and Results from Knowledge Workers.

But how do you know if your knowledge workers are pulling their full weight? You can't monitor their progress as you do workers on the line. Their work is intangible and often invisible: they're leveraging their individual expertise to make judgment calls, they're improvising, they're collaborating with others inside and outside your organization, they're working off-site, and they're cultivating relationships with customers. How do you know if you're managing them effectively?

How to Get More from Knowledge Workers

Because knowledge work is difficult to measure, some bosses take a laissez-faire approach: they don't "manage" their knowledge workers at all. Others impose traditional management practices on them—for example, telling them how to do their jobs or subjecting them to hierarchical reporting structures. Such techniques only backfire with people who know more than their supervisor does about their areas of expertise, who demand high levels of autonomy, and who thrive best when working with others in social networks.

Davenport maintains that managers of knowledge workers can get more from their people. One strategy is to provide them with technologies such as PDAs and instant messaging—and, most important, guidelines on how to use them effectively—which can enable them to communicate more efficiently with each other and with clients no matter where they're located. Another is to facilitate social networks through which high-performing workers can quickly find and share valuable information they need to move their projects forward. Even changes in physical workspace can help—such as augmenting a variety of collaborative spaces with quiet offices where workers can think privately without distraction.

But equally important, Davenport argues, managers of knowledge workers must play their role in new ways. He believes that, in the aggregate, these changes will constitute a managerial revolution.

From Boss to "Player/Coach"

Davenport predicts several key shifts in the management of knowledge workers. First, he contends that rather than simply overseeing work, managers of knowledge workers will increasingly come from the ranks of knowledge workers themselves, performing work similar to those whom they manage. Moreover, they will have very different priorities from past generations of managers. Instead of organizing hierarchies, they'll organize communities. And instead of hiring or firing workers, their job will center on developing and training them.

And rather than supporting the bureaucracy, he adds, knowledge-work managers will "fend it off in order to give their knowledge workers the freedom to do their best work." He notes that some of the greatest knowledge-work organizations in recent times—take the Manhattan Project and Xerox's Palo Alto Research Center (PARC) in California—have assigned senior executives the primary role of protecting knowledge workers from bureaucracy. Such executives fulfill this role through numerous means, for instance, by ensuring that adequate funds continue to flow into the right knowledge-work projects, by translating the content of knowledge work for other managers who don't understand it, and by parrying attempts to impose unnecessary structure on knowledge workers.

Many managers will find it difficult to strike just the right balance between overseeing knowledge workers and performing knowledge work alongside them, Davenport says. He acknowledges that this new type of knowledge-work boss, the so-called player/coach, feels constant tension. Focusing too much on your traditional managerial responsibilities, such as budgeting and planning, may mean losing touch with clients' and customers' real concerns. On the other hand, tipping the scale too far toward performing knowledge work may cause managerial responsibilities to suffer.

How do you resolve the tension? Many professional services firms, universities, and research organizations

Why Keeping Productivity High Is More Critical Now

Laissez-faire and out-of-date approaches to managing knowledge workers are especially damaging now that knowledge work can be "offshored" as readily as other types of work, Davenport says. Today, some companies are looking to countries such as China and India to perform their knowledge work. To justify keeping consulting, systems integration, product design, engineering, and other such work at home, companies must ensure that their knowledge workers are more productive than global competitors'. And that means managing them in new ways.

have long mastered the problem and offer models to emulate. For example, people at the executive level in a university "keep their hand in" knowledge work by continuing to teach, conduct research, and publish. But whatever the approach, "it needs to be developed at the organizational level," says Davenport. "A law firm might have some partners assigned to spend more time managing people, while others focus on serving clients. This requires organizational consensus, since those partners who mainly manage people will generate fewer billable hours." Some companies also rotate people through the two roles.

However, Davenport warns against removing people from knowledge-work activity—especially contact with clients and customers—for long periods. "These employees will lose other knowledge workers' respect if they're out of touch with the work for too long," he says.

Clarifying the Job's Meaning

In addition to mastering the player/coach role, Davenport says, a top priority for managers of knowledge workers is to "put the organization in context" for their employees. "Knowledge workers have a much higher need than other employees to feel that they're contributing to a larger whole and that their organization is doing meaningful work," he says. As he writes in *Thinking for a Living*, these workers "need to know the broader context in which they work: the industry direction, the company's positioning within the industry, key corporate initiatives, specific performance goals, and how the individual's performance relates to those factors."

Equally important, a manager needs to take great care in assigning his employees projects that they find both personally interesting and that align with the organization's goals. Finding the right fit here requires time and attention to detail. More give-and-take may be required in assigning and shaping assignments for knowledge workers compared with other employees. When workers feel ownership of their projects and see how they fit into the bigger picture, they will be that much more effective.

Measuring and Experimenting
with Performance

Knowledge-work managers also need to evaluate their people's performance in new ways, Davenport says. "Judge them on their outputs—their results—not their inputs, such as the number of hours they're working or where they're doing their work." Create quality measures. Even if these measures are subjective, they can be effective if they're broad enough. For example, at a professional services firm, the head of press and analyst relations might use "number of media mentions" and "favorable ratings in analysts' reports" as performance metrics.

Then experiment with changes designed to improve performance on the metrics you've defined. Managers shouldn't just make interventions in an effort to get more out of knowledge workers, Davenport says. "We also need to learn from how we intervene." Too many companies initiate changes—such as moving knowledge workers from closed offices into cubes in an attempt to generate more open communication—without evaluating the changes' impact on performance. "We're experimenting, but we're not learning from our experiments," says Davenport.

His advice? "Engineer less change but more intelligent change." Design experiments that change one thing at a time. For example, if you put people in facilities with a new office design, don't give them new information

> # Knowledge workers have a strong need to feel that their work contributes to the whole.

technologies to try at the same time. Also figure out how you're going to measure the impact of the change you've made. "You don't need a PhD in statistics," Davenport says. "But you do need to keep your experiments simple and disciplined."

Knowledge-intensive companies—those with the highest proportion of knowledge workers—are the fastest growing and most successful in the United States and other leading economies. By managing these workers in new ways, you boost your chances of extracting maximum value from them and sustaining your firm's momentum.

Reprint U0606C

Managing Leaders' Knowledge

• • •

Leaders' knowledge and experience play a unique role in a company's performance. Thus, developing—and then managing—what leaders know requires unique strategies. The articles in this section examine this subject. You'll find selections explaining the advantages that companies can gain by creating a "chief knowledge officer" role, strategies for developing future leaders in your team, and advice for establishing communities of best practice within which aspiring leaders can learn from their peers.

What the Chief Learning Officer Actually Knows

• • •

Loren Gary

You've heard the faddish talk: In the 21st century, more business will be based on intangibles. A company's most important assets will be not its factories or inventories, but the knowledge and experience of its people. News bulletin: For certain enlightened organizations, that future has already begun. These pioneers are exploring ways to treat knowledge management as a business process.

Knowledge management, according to Ellen Knapp of Coopers & Lybrand, is "the art of transforming intellectual assets into enduring value for an organization's clients and its people." Sounds great, but how do you do this? For many companies, part of the answer has been the creation of a new position, the chief learning officer, or CLO. This executive, who alternatively may go by the title chief knowledge officer or director of knowledge management, is not to be confused with the chief information officer, or CIO, who's responsible for the company's information technology (read "hardware and software"). The work of a chief learning officer, according to Knapp, who is both chief knowledge officer and a vice chair of her Big-Six firm, is "to make sure that the organization has the processes, the systems, and the culture to facilitate effective knowledge sharing—both within the organization and between the organization and its clients."

And what, precisely, does that entail? Conversations with real live CLOs lead us to five overarching conclusions. The details supporting them are best presented in the practitioners' own words, which, like the language of any set of people pioneering a new field, has its own distinctive set of charms and ineffabilities.

The new economic order is indeed upon us.

People like Peter Drucker and Lester Thurow have been writing about the coming knowledge revolution for years now. Perhaps more surprising, their quantitatively oriented brethren have not been far behind. William Bruns, Henry R. Byers Professor of Business Administration at Harvard Business School, notes that accountants have been searching for ways to make intellectual assets more measurable for decades. "We've had work done on human asset accounting for the past 30 years," he says, citing the 1974 book *Human Asset Accounting* by Eric Flamholtz as an example. "But the recognition that knowledge and intellect are the critically important ingredients in the economic equation is only just now being heard through the background noise," argues Alan Kantrow, chief knowledge officer at Monitor Company, a strategy consulting firm. The watershed, in this regard, may have been 1991. In that year, capital spending by U.S. companies for telecommunications and computer equipment for the first time exceeded corporate spending on industrial, construction, mining, and farming equipment. Since then, the lead maintained by new-economy investment has steadily widened. The increased emphasis on adding value through knowledge and innovation has now begun to extend beyond professional service firms, the consulting and accounting outfits where you'd most expect it, to companies in commodity and raw materials businesses. For example, Buckman Laboratories, a Memphis chemical manufacturer, has set up a department charged with knowledge transfer.

Brook Manville, a partner in the organization practice of McKinsey & Co., attributes the changes under way to several factors: "The globalization of business and its resultant competitiveness, as well as the fact that with companies now spread out across the world, it's harder to keep track of who knows what in an organization. The trend toward hard assets becoming commoditized. The way that increasingly transparent information calls for more innovation—as people realize just what's possible, they become choosier. These all have contributed to the appearance of a knowledge-based economy. More and more, companies need to have a distinct value proposition in order to survive."

Knapp even sees a link between this need to differentiate through knowledge management and "the end of the downsizing and reengineering era of the past 18 to 24 months." (You mean it's finally over?) "Now that we're out of the downsizing frenzy, we're more focused on growth and innovation," she explains. "So intellectual property and intellectual capital have taken on central importance."

All types of knowledge are not the same.

Or, as a CLO is more likely to put it, knowledge is multiple, and must be captured and transmitted in different ways. Kantrow draws a distinction among three types: know that, know why, and know how. "'Know that' is essentially data, statistics, facts. It's storable on disk, but when using it, you need to make sure you're comparing apples to apples. 'Know why' is the analytical understanding of causal sequences. For example, why did raising the price here affect demand there? This kind of knowledge is best captured in expert systems. The last type, 'know how,' is tacit knowledge, or craft knowledge. It can't be stored on a disk; rather, you have to apprentice to someone in order to learn it."

"If you want to develop an understanding of knowledge management that is both rigorous and deeply shared throughout the company," Kantrow advises, "you first need to build an awareness of what kinds and types of knowledge are relevant to which processes. And then you need to create a knowledge generation and capture process that enables you to plug the right pieces of knowledge into the right place."

Suppose, for example, you're designing a strategy to introduce a brand of toothpaste into Shanghai. You may know something about the different customer segments there, but there are probably other things about the market and the competition that you don't know. Effective knowledge management should help you determine whether an investment of additional resources to secure those knowledge assets would be worth the effort.

Nicholas Rudd, chief knowledge officer at Wunderman Cato Johnson, an ad agency subsidiary of Young & Rubicam, distinguishes between a geographic approach to knowledge management and one that looks at domains of knowledge central to the business everywhere. "We work with clients in 65 offices in some 35 countries around the world," he explains. "So we try to determine what has worked well in a client relationship in one region, and figure out how we can do things better the next time in that particular arena. When we look at domains of knowledge—say, customer loyalty—then anything that we can learn from around the globe about retaining a customer is valuable to us."

Fundamental to Rudd's work is fostering "the emergence of practice groups—informal networks of people who can abstract from their work with clients the principles and frameworks of theory that can be applied to future challenges." Somewhat similarly, Steve Kerr, vice president for corporate leadership development at General Electric, is engaged in supporting a companywide "six-sigma" quality initiative, which the company hopes will reduce defects in its business processes to three per million parts by the year 2000. Most of his efforts revolve around sharing best-practice information: setting up seminars, databases that can be accessed through the Internet, or creating other learning opportunities.

But CLOs also come to appreciate that what has worked best in specific situations in the past may not always be applicable going forward. Kantrow cautions that "when you're operating in complex and messy markets, where the context is overwhelmingly determinative, best-practice information—what Company X did in the Shanghai market—may not be all that relevant." The key is "to understand the relationship between different bits of knowledge and the strategic decision-making paths facing you, and to bring that knowledge to bear in a timely fashion."

The process of figuring out that relationship, and what knowledge the organization has available to it, can, to an outsider, look a lot like garden-variety consulting. Judy Lewis, information systems manager for the Knowledge Management Approach Program at Hewlett-Packard, describes what she does as akin to "peeling away the layers of an onion," to test hypotheses the organization may have about how it is, or should be, exploiting its knowledge. Her team partners with business units to focus particularly on how to generate new products.

A typical week has Lewis and her colleagues traveling from their Palo Alto base to conduct the next phase of a consultation that started six months earlier with one of HP's businesses, a printer manufacturer that accounts for 10% of the company's revenues. In the course of several days with the general manager of the unit and members of his staff, Lewis and her team will conduct a "knowledge assessment," trying to determine what the unit's needs and opportunities are. "In such cases, senior managers start with some fairly general goals for using their knowledge assets," Lewis explains. "They want to share more—they think. They want to collaborate more—they think. And they don't really know where to start in terms of addressing these issues."

The next step for Lewis and her team is to develop an interview process, working up and down the organizational ladder, verifying and refining the hunches the unit's leadership has presented them with. "It's a matter of being diligent about the questions," she says. "Then,

once the interviewing is complete, we'll create visual arti-
facts—maps, graphs, or some visual way of representing
what people have said to us—to present to the unit. The
people see where the gaps in their thinking or their
processes are." This particular project will continue for
several more months, but Lewis sees her program's
involvement with HP's business units as ongoing.
"We help a unit out with assessment, then move on to
the implementation, monitoring, and feedback phases.
Down the road, the unit may come back to us with a new
problem. So our involvement never really ends."

Effective knowledge management requires well-developed people skills.

McKinsey's Manville identifies several different components of knowledge management. Some lend themselves
to a systems approach—information management, for
example ("Let's put all that we know about this customer
into a fancy database."). But others do not: getting
people to learn faster, which requires an understanding
of individual development and team dynamics. Or align-
ing people so that they work better, which may call for
expertise in organizational design. Or managing relationships across a web of alliances. Here the skills required
look a lot more like those traditionally associated with a
human resource professional, a deft general manager, or
a first-class change agent.

"Resistance to new knowledge in an organization is natural," explains Steven Berglas, the director of Executive Development Resources and a clinical psychologist at Harvard Medical School. "In fact, a company's success often serves to reinforce what it does best, providing a disincentive to acquire new knowledge. Knowledge acquisition can only take place in an environment that's receptive and fertile"—that is, a climate in which the organization's prevailing attitudes about what needs to be done can be called into question, a climate that tolerates conflict. "Moreover, people learn, assimilate, and accept information at different speeds," Berglas continues. "The most important task for a CLO, therefore, is to manage conflict constructively and facilitate information exchange in a non-threatening way."

Whether the tools of knowledge management are applied to specific functional areas or across the entire company, they must be linked to strategy and business fundamentals—in measurable ways. Most companies still have a long way to go on this front.

Most CLOs tend to have a functional orientation to knowledge management, Knapp asserts—they apply knowledge management only to the technology or training sides of the business, or focus it on managing the company's portfolio of patents. "By contrast, there are very few places where knowledge management is understood to be part of the entire company's value proposition, and is integral to the overall business strategy." Without clear links to plans for serving internal or external customers better, or to beating the competition, the snazziest knowledge-capture system may seem mere trendy intellectual wheel spinning. The links to business fundamentals—new business generation, increased productivity, greater profitability, lower costs, faster delivery time—must be measurable in order to carry any weight.

The focus of knowledge management shouldn't be just inside the organization; there are tremendous opportunities for leveraging knowledge externally.

Use what you learn to develop new businesses. At Coopers & Lybrand, efforts to feed the heads of the firm's tax practitioners have led to the introduction of the Tax News Network, a Web-based product that offers a steady stream of information on the progress of tax-related legislation, with subscription services and private channels available for additional fees. "We've basically come up with a way of creating a town meeting within the tax director community while the legislation is being crafted," Knapp says proudly.

As must be clear from this brief survey, the field of knowledge management is still very much in its infancy, especially when it comes to developing metrics and valuation methods that would command the respect of an auditor or investor. But the work has begun. And can your organization, if it doesn't have a chief learning officer, afford to wait until the job of quantification is further along? Your most precious 21st century asset may be wasting.

Reprint U9612A

The Art of Developing Leaders

• • •

Vijay Vishwanath and Marcia Blenko

Of the handful of CEOs who were rumored last spring to be on the short list for the top job at Coca-Cola, three share strikingly similar backgrounds. Mattel's Robert Eckert, Hershey's Richard Lenny, and Gillette's Jim Kilts all cut their managerial teeth at Kraft General Foods.

That's no coincidence. During the past two decades, Kraft has been a prodigious producer of big cheeses. In addition to playing the leading role at Mattel, Hershey, and Gillette, Kraft alumni have held the top posts at Sears, Quaker Oats, Campbell Soup, Young & Rubicam, and Marks & Spencer. And while GE may get a lot of credit for graduating leaders to other organizations, Kraft has become a CEO machine.

The secret lies in Kraft's management development process. In many firms, development programs are run in carefully controlled hothouses, apart from the daily work of the organization. Executives enroll in a series of topical courses or undertake an intensive study of case material. But when you grow leaders in a hothouse, you end up with hothouse flowers: they look perfectly good, but they wilt when exposed to the elements.

At Kraft, leadership development isn't an isolated process. Though the company does have a formal program for training leaders, for the most part executive development takes place on the job and, more important, for the job. Throughout, it's designed to reinforce Kraft's business model. Building brands is critical to Kraft's success. Other consumer-products companies separate brand building from cost reduction, but at Kraft the two are linked: reducing costs systematically lets the company invest in strengthening brands—and general managers are expected to be adept at both.

As promising managers advance, they face a series of challenges through which they learn to apply that model in varying circumstances. Beginning with their earliest assignments, they're expected to demonstrate the kind of sophisticated thinking that's usually found only within the top tiers of executives at most companies. As managers ascend the ranks, Kraft encourages them to

develop a set of conceptual and interpersonal skills critical to corporate leaders—such as creativity, the power to
persuade and influence, and the willingness to take risks.
Perhaps most distinguishing of all, the Kraft process
gives young executives extraordinarily broad authority
that stretches their abilities and spurs their growth.

Behind the success of Kraft's leadership development
process you'll find a set of principles that any company
can learn from.

Focus on the big picture from the start.

The dominant development principle in a Kraft manager's early years is "bottom-line responsibility." This
ties in to the bedrock idea of the company's business
model: that cost reduction is not a one-time, reactive
program but rather an ongoing strategic process for
freeing up cash to invest in marketing. Cost cutting, in
other words, provides the fuel for brand building.

That broader scope can be seen clearly in the roles and
titles Kraft gives its up-and-coming managers. Most
consumer-products companies assign fledgling executives posts as "brand managers" that focus heavily on advertising initiatives aimed at boosting sales. Kraft calls
such executives "category business directors" and makes
them responsible for much more than just marketing.

At this early stage, Kraft encourages rising managers
to concentrate on building a deep understanding of the

Kraft's Secret Recipe

A set of five guiding principles drives Kraft's remarkably successful approach to developing leaders:

1. **Focus on the big picture.** Unlike most consumer-products companies, Kraft gives its up-and-comers bottom-line responsibility right from the start.

2. **Give managers the freedom to take action.** Once young managers have mastered the basics of the business, they are given unusually broad leeway in deciding how to meet their targets.

3. **School managers in the art of influence, not issuing orders.** Kraft develops the art of influence in its managers, preparing them to get work done through others across the entire company.

4. **Discourage self-promotion.** Kraft nurtures collective achievement, not the desire to be in the spotlight.

5. **Find the right home for talent.** Not everyone can lead the company, but Kraft has a commitment to keep talented people onboard and has created roles for value creators who are not made to be leaders.

supply side. They're called on to deal with commodity markets, manufacturing, and cash management on a day-to-day basis.

According to current and former Kraft executives, it isn't unusual for category business directors to find themselves out in the middle of agricultural fields talking to farmers or down on factory floors troubleshooting a production glitch with machine operators.

As a result, young managers gain the ability to talk to customers about the entirety of Kraft's business, including the supply chain and the manufacturing operation. If, for instance, there's a short-term product shortage, the managers can discuss the causes of the problem in depth with their customers—and find a solution that ensures the buyers' continued satisfaction.

To drive home to executives their responsibility for cost control, Kraft ties their pay and incentives to overall profit performance. That's another striking way Kraft differs from traditional consumer-products firms, which tend to compensate young executives for achieving targeted revenue gains with little regard to cost management. "Back in 1983 and 1984, when I was running margarine at Kraft," recalls Hershey's Richard Lenny, "I had more skin in the game than many managers get over a lifetime." From the start, Kraft works to create general managers— future CEOs with the ability to see the big picture.

Allow freedom of action to foster initiative and creativity.

Once young managers have developed a thorough overview of the business, Kraft lets them take action. Though the company imposes tough financial objectives, it gives managers enormous leeway in figuring out the best way to hit their targets.

Former Kraft CFO Gary Coughlan says that the approach reduces bureaucracy and encourages personal

> Leaving room for experimentation, including the occasional misstep, is the right way to grow effective leaders.

initiative. "If you did the job right, you didn't have to write a lot of memos," he recalls. "Once you showed your competence, you were left alone, and you were then able to develop your own style."

Leaving room for experimentation, including the occasional misstep, is the right way to grow effective leaders, Kraft believes. Consider this story from Gillette's Jim Kilts. Early in his career, when Kilts was running a cheese unit, his biggest challenge was the threat posed by private-label brands, which had begun capturing significant market share. Given the freedom to determine the best course of action and implement it quickly, he decided to provide retailers with promotional incentives, assuming they'd pass the savings along to customers in the form of lower prices. As it turned out, however, the retailers kept the cash without reducing prices—continuing to put Kraft's cheese at a disadvantage to the private labels.

So Kilts changed course and reduced the list prices of his products, providing the cuts directly to consumers. He had made a mistake, but it was a justifiable one, and he remedied it quickly. "You were allowed to make smart mistakes but not dumb ones," he recalls, "and you were

> Management development at Kraft does not hinge on identifying and nurturing "leadership personalities."

expected to make course corrections rapidly when something went wrong."

Although other consumer products companies allow top executives freedom of action, Kraft pushes that concept down deep into its organization, well into the ranks of middle management, liberating managers to constantly try out new ways to improve the company. Such latitude acts as a magnet for talent. Doug Conant, now at Campbell Soup, says that environment drew him to Kraft. "You were expected to grow the top line, bottom line, and market share, but there was more freedom to operate," he notes.

School managers in the art of influence, not issuing orders.

At Kraft, functions such as marketing and manufacturing overlap the product units, and the company moves executives thoughtfully between line and staff posts. The approach is geared not only to broaden the knowledge base of up-and-coming executives but also to produce function heads with the perspective and skills of strong general managers.

The goal is to create leaders who are thoroughly dexterous at both making and influencing decisions. As line operators, they learn to call the play judiciously, and by involving staff they become more skilled at working through others, a leadership ability that's become critical in an era of flat organizations.

The executives in charge of categories and brands cannot simply issue imperatives; they must learn to use persuasion and build consensus. As one former executive puts it, "You often had a lot of people sitting around a table—and if you were going to be successful, you needed those people to deliver. So learning how to motivate them without the authority to control their careers was important."

As evidence of Kraft's commitment to moving managers around its matrix of staff and line jobs, former co-CEO Betsy Holden points out that Kraft's top executives have more than 20 years of experience with the company on average, yet usually have been in their current roles for only two years.

The unusual career path taken by Ed Smeds is typical. A staffer who started in human resources, Smeds became CFO for Kraft and then made a jump over to the line, as general manager for Australia and then Canada. Before retiring, he moved back to the staff side to run purchasing and logistics. The strong staff functions provide a balance and a foil to the line executives, and Kraft has deliberately filled staff positions with individuals who often come from the line.

Discourage self-promotion and self-interest.

Management development at Kraft does not hinge on identifying and nurturing "leadership personalities." In fact, long before Jim Collins came forward with his research on the dangers of charismatic company heads in *Good to Great: Why Some Companies Make the Leap . . . and Others Don't*, Kraft recognized the importance of "lack of hubris" as a leadership quality. Unlike his counterparts at other leading companies, Mike Miles, the former CEO of Kraft, was rarely seen on magazine covers in the '80s and early '90s.

Self-promoters need not apply at Kraft. The company promotes leadership not as a personality cult but as an ingrained habit of putting the company's interests first and helping colleagues succeed. The aim is to create an environment that nurtures collective achievement, not to breed executives who crave the spotlight. Recalls Bob Morrison, a Kraft alumnus who went on to head Quaker Oats, "We weren't hot dogs. We just tried to do things a little better every day."

Move stalled talent over, not out.

Of course, not everyone is able to advance successfully to the top of Kraft's leadership development program. Instead of letting go of experienced business managers, however, Kraft often moves them into staff functions. Indeed, the top management of the company is committed to creating "staff slots" to keep strong talent onboard.

Kraft's former HR chief John Tucker, one of the architects of the leadership track, recalls a telling example: "One [staffer] was a vice president in strategy—smart as a whip. And there was a lot of discussion as to whether she could make it in a general manager position. At the end of the day, we made her president of one of the businesses within Kraft.

"We knew that business had a strong infrastructure and staff. It wasn't going to hell in a hand basket. And I went in once a month to check in—to keep a finger on the pulse. After about a year, it was obvious to all of us that it wasn't going to work. And we brought her back into strategy, where she was even better than before having had that experience."

That policy ensures that Kraft doesn't lose the investment it makes in its people. And by providing a safety net to executives on the leadership track, it further encourages them to test their wings through experimentation with new ideas and risk-taking.

Can other companies follow Kraft's lead? Yes and no. Management development at Kraft is tailored to the company's business model, so it would be a mistake to try to replicate it blindly; what's right for Kraft is unlikely to be right for another company.

But it is possible to adopt the basic approach. Any company can think carefully about its business model and the principles underpinning it. Any company can chart a career course for managers that reinforces those principles. And any company can give its young executives the responsibility to think and act like well-rounded chief executives.

Reprint U0411B

Five Questions About Peer-to-Peer Leadership Development

• • •

The role of communities of practice in helping employees develop competence and technical expertise has been well documented. But the animating idea behind CompanyCommand.com—a Web site that serves as a professional forum for Army officers at the first level of command authority—is the belief that a community of practice can do even more: it can provide those who are in the middle of a leadership challenge with real-time connections to people who have had similar experiences.

And those connections, say U.S. Army majors Tony Burgess, Nate Allen, Pete Kilner, and Steve Schweitzer, as well as knowledge-management consultant Nancy Dixon—members of the Web site's team—can be transformative.

1. What makes a community of practice so powerful?

Burgess: In January, we received an e-mail from a Lieutenant Stephanie in Iraq. On her first day as a personnel officer, her battalion lost its first soldier. She hadn't been trained yet in how to handle such an occurrence, but she needed to act fast and to show her battalion that she knew what to do. Given the sensitive nature of the issue, she wasn't comfortable asking just anyone for help.

We got an e-mail conversation going that brought the power of the profession to bear on Lt. Stephanie's situation. In short order, not only did she have a sample letter of condolence to the dead soldier's family, she had an example of how one commander had put together a memorial service and a wealth of advice about how to proceed with all the applicable Army regulations.

2. She got the resources she needed fast. What's so special about that?

Dixon: She got a lot more than resources. The conversation that developed helped her contextualize her learning. Conversation is a much more powerful vehicle for learning because it's demand driven rather than supply driven. Through conversation, Lt. Stephanie was able to get advice that was tailored to her particular context. When the people you're talking with understand your situation because they've been there themselves, it creates the possibility for a kind of learning that a database or book can't begin to match.

3. How does this kind of learning make you a better leader?

Schweitzer: You learn how to lead not primarily through formal instruction but in the course of reflecting with others in your profession on the concrete challenges you face.

Leadership has three components: knowing, doing, and being. Most organizations are pretty good at teaching people what they need to know and how to do what they're supposed to in order to excel. The *being* part is where many organizations fall down; that's where a community of practice comes in.

4. How so?

Kilner: Learning how to lead is not just a cognitive process; there's also an affective element. Who you learn from is just as important as what you learn: two people can give me the same advice, but I'll be more receptive to the advice coming from the one who has actually been in the same circumstances I'm facing. Only by making a connection with others who've shared your experience can some lessons become a part of your art—a part of who you are.

So at the same time that Lt. Stephanie was learning how to respond to the death of one of her soldiers, she was also learning something about leadership from the way people in the community of practice interacted with her and took care of her. By building the connections that allow modeling and tacit learning to take place, CompanyCommand.com was helping her learn how to be a leader.

5. Are you suggesting that it isn't important for an organization to carefully articulate its core values?

Allen: No, it's just that trying to push a set of approved values down through the ranks isn't very effective. If we advertised our Web site as a place where people could get help with their values, we wouldn't get many hits. Instead, we focus on helping commanders improve their competence. In doing that, we earn their trust—only then does a dialogue about values become possible.

Reprint U0412F

Leveraging Knowledge Management Technology

. . .

Technology can play a vital role in knowledge management. But technology in itself isn't enough; managers must use it effectively. The articles in this section examine this theme more closely. You'll find selections describing the benefits that a Web-based knowledge-management system can generate, explaining how to build a KM portal, and offering suggestions for extracting the most value from your KM technology.

The New Uses
of Intranets

. . .

Y2K has come and gone, and corporate IT departments
are turning their attention to that perennial technological stepchild, the intranet. Their findings? Good internal
Web sites—intranets—can be powerful tools for information sharing and knowledge management of all sorts.
"The intranet is the communications platform for
group work—the 'electronic brain' employees tap into,"
says Steve McCormick, a consultant with Watson Wyatt
Worldwide's Washington, D.C. office and the lead
author of the firm's fourth annual report on "e-HR."

What's new here isn't groupware, which Lotus Notes
broke ground on a decade ago. The novelty is putting
everything on the same Web-based system. As Elizabeth
Grover, HR VP at Veritas Software, puts it, "With so

many people using the Web in everyday life, why would you do anything different at work?"

The intranet at Aventis Cambridge Genomics Center, an arm of the European life-sciences giant Aventis, has some widely used features. Supplemented by a software package called PharMatrix, it features distributed usage with varied levels of security, centralized file storage, document check-in and check-out, change alerts, newsgroups, threaded e-mail discussions, and the ability to add URLs and to link databases. Still, nobody's intranet is really typical. "People use technology for different things," says Tim Duncan, president of First Call Interactive, a builder of intranets for financial services clients that is part of Thomson Financial. "I don't think anyone knows what intranets really are. They see different parts of the elephant."

This lack of definition leads many companies to make unwise intranet investments, Duncan says. "Intranets are very much a hot thing; people are throwing money at them. But they're not thinking carefully a lot of the time about how information should be used." First Call Interactive, for example, avoids building companywide intranets, focusing instead on a key item for one specific group, such as customer lists for a sales force. "You have to have a brain behind all this. Everybody has decided they need a library, but they're not hiring a librarian," he says.

Get a brain in place, though, and there's a lot a well-designed intranet can do. For example:

Keep People in Touch

At MadeToOrder.com, a seller of corporate logo apparel, the intranet is the key to efficient functioning of the company's newly created—and widely distributed—workforce. The intranet allows "remote employees to feel part of the company," says president and CEO Weston Rose. Intranets hardly remove the need for face-to-face interaction, but—paradoxically—they can improve on-site gatherings. "The meetings you do have are more meaningful; you don't have to spend a lot of time catching up."

Facilitate Training and Knowledge Sharing

A favorite intranet site of JCPenney managers is the company's Knowledge Management System, which is used for interactive training and distance learning. After signing in, each manager views a desktop customized by the manager's function and level. The desktops contain training programs and management tips. "We don't publish or mail training materials any longer," says Deborah Masten, director of HR communications and development at Penney's corporate headquarters. That's a huge savings for a far-flung retailer that hires between 400 and 700 management trainees a year.

Intranets: Where Is Your Company?

The development of a company's intranet typically moves through four distinct phases, says Steve McCormick, a consultant with Watson Wyatt Worldwide's Washington, D.C. office:

Phase One: posting documents such as policy manuals on an internal Web site.

Phase Two: providing access to personal data such as benefits selections.

Phase Three: enabling one-way transactions such as changing retirement accounts.

Phase Four: employee-to-employee information sharing. That's what's taking place at many companies now, says McCormick. "Once you get documents, data, and transactions online, companies begin to realize that the Web is a community knowledge tool."

Another useful feature: asynchronous discussion. Penney managers can ask questions of their peer group, and other managers can answer when they log in. All Q&As are automatically stored for future reference. More than 500 managers use the Knowledge Management System daily, with some 300 entering the discussion groups.

Automate Routine Tasks

"At Microsoft, we're doing everything on the intranet," says Mary Lee Kennedy, director of information services at the software company's headquarters. Microsoft's intranet contains about 1,000 sites, more than two million pages, and dozens of applications and functionalities. Every day, roughly a third of the company's 30,000 employees log on to MSWeb, the most general-purpose site. Another favorite: MSMarket, an intranet where employees can buy office supplies and book travel tickets. The site is a time-saver for employees and a purchasing department's dream, seamlessly integrating vendors. Kennedy: "I don't have to fill out any paperwork to do my job. It's e-commerce, inside the company."

Provide Easy Access to Information

Four years ago, managers at Kraft Foods saw a need to coordinate Web usage among different company divisions. "All the groups were developing Web pages at the same time. We wanted to make sure that not all of them were reinventing the wheel and duplicating effort," recalls Karen Isaacson, director of HR information and technology at the company's headquarters. Kraft set up an intranet committee composed of representatives from corporate affairs, HR, legal, and IT. The result: the Kraft Intranet Café, a striking Web site that is the default home page for every Kraft employee. The café gives users easy access to the rest of the company's intranet sites, such as HR Online.

Cut Overhead Costs

Storage-management software maker Veritas uses the intranet to reduce administrative costs. "The reality is that we [in HR] are overhead. We have to think of ways of doing things better and reducing the percentage of overall costs that HR accounts for," says HR VP Grover. She began by putting basic HR information on the intranet, then added a Web application that managers use to figure merit raises. The intranet version of the merit calculations contains several improvements over the spreadsheets Grover formerly sent to managers, and at the same time streamlines HR's involvement. "It didn't cut down on the time managers spent on salary pools much, but it dramatically cut down on HR time," she says. She seeks similar improvements with a plan to add Veritas's stock grant calculations to the intranet later this year.

Organize—and Communicate—Data

For many industries, the need to manage data goes beyond a nicety. "Our premise is that instead of not enough information, there's too much information," says Hal Roberts, an engineer with First Call Interactive. "Ten years ago any financial services company would do all that it could to get more information. The trick now is finding the right information quickly." Intranets linked to several databases can organize the voluminous material. "A huge part of the value [of intranets] is in the interface—in taking whatever info clients are already getting and making it easier to find," he says.

For example, Kraft and JCPenney both use their intranets to coordinate sales efforts in ways that would have been more cumbersome and costly before the advent of the Web. Penney managers can look at sales reports through the company's Infovision intranet site, and can share information (such as slow-seller reports) with peer groups through the Knowledge Management System. Kraft's sales force, often on the road, can log in remotely to divisional intranet sites and generate sales reports "down to the granular level," says Isaacson.

Win-Win Marketing

MadeToOrder.com creates intranet sites for its clients free of charge, allowing the clients' employees to order corporate-logo shirts, hats, and so on with a few clicks. MadeToOrder gets the orders; clients get control over the use of their logo, which for many companies is a nagging problem. "This is a service that most corporations spend millions of dollars on," says CEO Rose. Several clients, including Symantec and the national YMCA organization, use the service.

Reprint U0005B

The Right Data at the Right Fingertips

• • •

Frank Steinfield

The dramatic and thus far wildly successful transformation of Krispy Kreme from a regional favorite in the southeast United States to a North America–wide phenomenon is well documented. But not so the role that knowledge management (KM) has played in the company's remarkable growth.

Indeed, Krispy Kreme's ability to at once compile and redistribute time-sensitive operational data through its dynamic KM portal, mykrispykreme.com, has been at the center of its ultrafast deployment of new outposts. And this strategic use of KM is emblematic of how innovative companies are employing their knowledge assets to grow revenue and cut costs. Whether streamlining a franchise system, unlocking additional value from a merger, or centralizing information for reuse by engagement teams, companies such as Krispy Kreme, Millennium Pharmaceuticals, and PricewaterhouseCoopers that understand how and when to deploy different KM components are finding that now more than ever this once-heralded and then all-but-forgotten practice can directly improve business.

Search and Deploy

Krispy Kreme's store managers were collecting all the data the firm needed to open and run highly efficient outposts—for instance, hourly doughnut production by store and responses to current promotions—but the information was so dispersed across the organization that the company was unable to "convert it to something actionable," says Krispy Kreme's chief information officer, Frank Hood. Realizing that the company's demanding growth plans depended on this changing quickly, Hood led the development of a continually updated knowledge management portal through which store managers could submit their own activity reports as well as access that treasure trove of data from other stores that had previously been all but unavailable.

Built on a platform of vanilla Web-based applications, the portal became a breakthrough tool for managers.

"It's a one-stop shop for the things they need to know to run the business," says Hood. Without such a tool, the effective transfer of best practices from one store to the next—a critical element in a fast-growing franchise business and something at which Krispy Kreme has come to excel—would have been crippled. No less importantly, the portal also allowed top management to gain a much more immediate—and more telling—view of key facets of the organization.

Where to Begin

While a sophisticated KM initiative may encompass myriad practices and applications deployed across a complex global organization, every effective KM effort begins with a rather simple conversation. KM guru Laurence Prusak, coauthor with Thomas H. Davenport and H. James Wilson of *What's the Big Idea? Creating and Capitalizing on the Best Management Thinking*, explains: "People should sit down within a group, a unit, a division, depending on the size of the firm, and say, 'What knowledge do we have? What knowledge is private that should be public? What knowledge don't we have that we want to have?' And then they should figure out an operational strategy to get there."

At Krispy Kreme, discussions centered on those questions led to the creation of the enterprise portal. As the core of the company's KM effort, the portal helps to accelerate and simplify a range of business processes such as sharing new product information, viewing floor plans, ordering equipment, and generating financials. But its value goes beyond direct store management. Authorized users of the portal have access to financial data as well as such marketing information as branding guidelines, drive-time radio excerpts, streaming video, and even the philosophy behind Krispy Kreme's marketing efforts.

Integrating KM throughout Krispy Kreme's business has also provided the company with a sharper focus on the big picture. "We leverage KM the most through forecasting and planning for that next big thing, that next branch of expansion," Hood says. "Information is important to look at from a forensic level if you're trying to find out why something didn't go right. We look at information more to plan how to make it go right in the future." Along with better access to data, Hood identifies a philosophical shift in people's attitudes: "We've created an environment where we can no longer do without that information."

Putting Together the Knowledge Pieces

In the pharmaceutical industry, where the product stems directly from the knowledge available to its creators, the ability to capture fast-moving data and integrate it across multiple disciplines is critical. Disease research requires you "to put together a very, very complicated jigsaw puzzle," says Joseph Horvath, director of KM at Millennium Pharmaceuticals. "The problem is the pieces don't all reside on your card table, they reside on card tables all over the world—in public databases, journal articles, and unpublished research findings." To help make it easier for researchers to find the right puz-

> "What you're going to see is not stuff that is labeled KM success. What you are going to see is stuff that is labeled better execution and strategy."

zle pieces, Millennium built a KM structure that provides an integrated view of both the external literature and the internal data. Delivering to scientists more complete, searchable, even computable information sets is essential to effective decision making in this industry where a company's ability to predict the probability of a drug's success far downstream is the key driver of return on investment.

Quickly coordinating complex information is also paying off in Millennium's approach to restructuring, mergers, and acquisitions. These conditions often require a company to rapidly evaluate its information and knowledge assets, from lab notebooks and electronic databases to the less tangible know-how associated with past projects, partnerships, and key technologies. Without oversight, these assets can evaporate—getting buried in off-site warehouses or leaving with departing employees. Even if assets are to be "shopped" outside the company, retaining the associated documents and know-how can be important to securing their market value.

"How do you make sure that before people leave you extract their tacit knowledge . . . like what's all this stuff in the lab refrigerator?" Horvath asks. "Well, at a pharma company, it's not yogurt and lunch, it's cell lines and reagents and expensive stuff that might not be well labeled or well indexed." Millennium has used organizational discipline around KM to extract the fullest possible value during its recent restructuring. This has meant engaging people affected by the changes early in the process, building knowledge retention surveys into the exit process, and even charting the departure dates of key people. "People care about the posterity of their work, particularly in the life sciences," says Horvath. "They don't feel like they're being exploited by a debriefing—they feel like the company cares about their work."

Streaming Knowledge

At PricewaterhouseCoopers (PwC), KM is helping to address one of the most pressing concerns of executives in the information economy: how to increase the productivity of knowledge workers—in this case, professionals in the firm's tax, assurance, and advisory practices. For example, as a decisive part of this effort, PwC's central tax KM group has created online Communities of Practice for several different tax areas, the focal points of which are compilations of relevant data in the form of issue-based tool kits. The tool kits, which include technical background, expert referrals, and quality and risk management assessment, not only help professionals identify important issues but also help create potential solutions to meet client needs. With the increased productivity stemming from having a single access point for such a wide range of problem-solving data, PwC estimates that the tool kits should bring $25 million to the bottom line over the next 12 months, says Christopher Cipriano, PricewaterhouseCoopers' partner in charge of U.S. KM.

But even when KM initiatives match corporate strategy and include incentives and good training, how do you ensure that people will use a new system in a large, complex organization? Making people change the way they work is difficult enough. When you're also introducing an entirely new software platform—which is often the case with KM initiatives—you're making things doubly tough. Recognizing this, PwC built its KM system on a platform that was already familiar to the workforce, creating a taxonomy for 20 existing databases driven by a customized search engine. "With our current infrastructure, we weren't able to search across databases, just within databases. We took it to the next level by linking up these databases and allowing people to search multiple databases at one time," says Cipriano.

With the help of intelligence from the front line, leading companies such as Krispy Kreme, Millennium Pharmaceuticals, and PricewaterhouseCoopers are locating sweet spots where KM streamlines operations, supports M&A, and improves client service. There is "substantial, non-sexy, abiding merit" in KM, according to Alan Kantrow, chief knowledge officer for the Monitor Group. "What you're going to see is not stuff that is labeled KM success. What you are going to see is stuff that is labeled better execution and strategy."

Reprint U0401C

Communication Technology That's Worth a Second Look

• • •

Eric Marcus

Some crucial communications technologies are finally able to add to the bottom line. You need to investigate these technologies with an eye to seeing how you can create competitive advantage with them.

Your Personal Internet

When you launch your Web browser, your personalized version of Yahoo! or the *Wall Street Journal* appears on your screen. But in this context, all "personalized" really means is that you checked some boxes when you started the service indicating what predefined content you want to see and in what format.

Soon, the Internet will offer each of us a truly unique view reflecting our individual interests. Not limited to just predefined selections, this new Internet will develop an understanding of what we like based on what we access, our location, and many other attributes. It will then select and format content to display just what we want to see, when we want to see it.

What's the opportunity? Why not form an association of companies that can offer a suite of services that are individually tailored to a client's needs? For example, you could link an airline (and its frequent flier miles) to the client's favorite hotel chain, rental car agency, and so on, to form a personalized travel site that would take today's travel dot-coms one step further toward true personalization.

Knowledge Sharing and Management

Very few companies have figured out how to get more than a handful of employees to invest any real effort in today's knowledge management systems. As a result, they become inert repositories of outdated information—an expensive waste of time.

A major European bank has developed an innovative solution to the knowledge-sharing dilemma. The bank changed the front end of its intranet to a graphical interface that looked like a village. Buildings reflected the various aspects of the bank's business. Within each building, lobby marquees identified what "discussions" were taking place on each floor, and then, on each floor marquees identified the "discussions" going on in each room. All employees were invited to see and experience the village.

Initially, employees visited the intranet just to see what all the talk was about. Then use began to grow. Soon, employees indicated that their primary motivation for going to the intranet was the sense of achievement they got from solving problems, in many cases with people they had never met.

Real-Time Communications

Imagine that you are working on a critical proposal when an expert you would have played "telephone tag" with in the past sends you an instant message that you immediately incorporate into the document. Millions of employees have already discovered that instant messaging (e.g., AOL Time Warner's IM, ICQ, and MSN Messenger) is quicker and easier than e-mail or the phone. International Data Corporation recently forecast that instant messenger users will increase from 18.4 million in 2001 to 229.2 million in 2005. There is already more data traffic in our networks than voice. Soon, there will be more machine-to-machine communications than human-to-human.

What other new services will organizations create by leveraging these capabilities? Companies with mobile assets (e.g., trucks, train cars, and containers) can know where they are at all times. Suppliers can enhance their relationships with buyers by creating smart, wireless, automatic reordering systems. Dematerializing the wire creates all kinds of new opportunities—how will your organization put them to use?

Computer-Directed Search, Customer Service, Bidding, and Quoting

When you do an Internet search for a diamond ring using Google, Excite, or AltaVista, you are using a software agent. Agents are just helpers that we ask to perform tasks for us. Another use of agents today is to find the lowest price for a product, such as a CD.

Today, software agents are used to provide information, compare pricing, and even accept orders. Soon software agents will:

- initiate and facilitate collaboration;

- cross-sell products and services; and

- transact business from sourcing through making payment.

Technology amplifies, but does not replace, face-to-face communications. Companies that figure out how to use these communication technologies to tie customer, need, and solution closer together will be the winners in the marketplace in the coming decade.

Reprint C0202D

About the Contributors

Tom Davenport is President's Distinguished Professor of Information Technology & Management at Babson. He has authored, coauthored, or edited 11 books—7 with HBS Press. Two of the books have been best-sellers.

Mattison Crowe is a contributor to *Harvard Management Update*.

David Boath is a partner in Accenture's Health & Life Sciences practice.

David Y. Smith is a partner at Accenture Learning.

Diane McFerrin Peters is a lecturer and consultant based in Harrisburg, Pennsylvania. She is coauthor (with Hal F. Rosenbluth) of *The Customer Comes Second* and *Care to Compete? Secrets from America's Best Companies on How to Manage with People and Profits in Mind*.

Rebecca M. Saunders is a contributor to *Harvard Management Update*.

Lauren Keller Johnson is a contributor to *Harvard Management Update*.

David Stauffer is a Montana-based business writer.

Loren Gary is a contributor to *Harvard Management Update*.

About the Contributors

Vijay Vishwanath directs Bain & Company's global consumer products practice.

Marcia Blenko is a leader in Bain's global organization practice.

Frank Steinfield is a consultant who uses communications to promote organizational change.

Eric Marcus is president of Corporate Alchemy, Inc., a management consulting firm based in Lincolnshire, Illinois.

Harvard Business Review Paperback Series

The Harvard Business Review Paperback Series offers the best thinking on cutting-edge management ideas from the world's leading thinkers, researchers, and managers. Designed for leaders who believe in the power of ideas to change business, these books will be useful to managers at all levels of experience, but especially senior executives and general managers. In addition, this series is widely used in training and executive development programs.

These books are priced at US$19.95
Price subject to change.

Title	Product #
Harvard Business Review **Interviews with CEOs**	3294
Harvard Business Review on **Advances in Strategy**	8032
Harvard Business Review on **Appraising Employee Performance**	7685
Harvard Business Review on **Becoming a High Performance Manager**	1296
Harvard Business Review on **Brand Management**	1445
Harvard Business Review on **Breakthrough Leadership**	8059
Harvard Business Review on **Breakthrough Thinking**	181X
Harvard Business Review on **Building Personal and Organizational Resilience**	2721
Harvard Business Review on **Business and the Environment**	2336
Harvard Business Review on **The Business Value of IT**	9121
Harvard Business Review on **Change**	8842
Harvard Business Review on **Compensation**	701X
Harvard Business Review on **Corporate Ethics**	273X
Harvard Business Review on **Corporate Governance**	2379
Harvard Business Review on **Corporate Responsibility**	2748
Harvard Business Review on **Corporate Strategy**	1429
Harvard Business Review on **Crisis Management**	2352
Harvard Business Review on **Culture and Change**	8369
Harvard Business Review on **Customer Relationship Management**	6994
Harvard Business Review on **Decision Making**	5572

To order, call 1-800-668-6780, or go online at www.HBSPress.org

Title	Product #
Harvard Business Review on **Developing Leaders**	5003
Harvard Business Review on **Doing Business in China**	6387
Harvard Business Review on **Effective Communication**	1437
Harvard Business Review on **Entrepreneurship**	9105
Harvard Business Review on **Finding and Keeping the Best People**	5564
Harvard Business Review on **Innovation**	6145
Harvard Business Review on **The Innovative Enterprise**	130X
Harvard Business Review on **Knowledge Management**	8818
Harvard Business Review on **Leadership**	8834
Harvard Business Review on **Leadership at the Top**	2756
Harvard Business Review on **Leadership in a Changed World**	5011
Harvard Business Review on **Leading in Turbulent Times**	1806
Harvard Business Review on **Managing Diversity**	7001
Harvard Business Review on **Managing High-Tech Industries**	1828
Harvard Business Review on **Managing People**	9075
Harvard Business Review on **Managing Projects**	6395
Harvard Business Review on **Managing the Value Chain**	2344
Harvard Business Review on **Managing Uncertainty**	9083
Harvard Business Review on **Managing Your Career**	1318
Harvard Business Review on **Marketing**	8040
Harvard Business Review on **Measuring Corporate Performance**	8826
Harvard Business Review on **Mergers and Acquisitions**	5556
Harvard Business Review on **Mind of the Leader**	6409
Harvard Business Review on **Motivating People**	1326
Harvard Business Review on **Negotiation**	2360
Harvard Business Review on **Nonprofits**	9091
Harvard Business Review on **Organizational Learning**	6153
Harvard Business Review on **Strategic Alliances**	1334
Harvard Business Review on **Strategies for Growth**	8850
Harvard Business Review on **Teams That Succeed**	502X
Harvard Business Review on **Turnarounds**	6366
Harvard Business Review on **What Makes a Leader**	6374
Harvard Business Review on **Work and Life Balance**	3286

To order, call 1-800-668-6780, or go online at www.HBSPress.org

Harvard Business Essentials

In the fast-paced world of business today, everyone needs a personal resource—a place to go for advice, coaching, background information, or answers. The Harvard Business Essentials series fits the bill. Concise and straightforward, these books provide highly practical advice for readers at all levels of experience. Whether you are a new manager interested in expanding your skills or an experienced executive looking to stay on top, these solution-oriented books give you the reliable tips and tools you need to improve your performance and get the job done. Harvard Business Essentials titles will quickly become your constant companions and trusted guides.

These books are priced at US$19.95, except as noted.
Price subject to change.

Title	Product #
Harvard Business Essentials: **Negotiation**	1113
Harvard Business Essentials: **Managing Creativity and Innovation**	1121
Harvard Business Essentials: **Managing Change and Transition**	8741
Harvard Business Essentials: **Hiring and Keeping the Best People**	875X
Harvard Business Essentials: **Finance for Managers**	8768
Harvard Business Essentials: **Business Communication**	113X
Harvard Business Essentials: **Manager's Toolkit ($24.95)**	2896
Harvard Business Essentials: **Managing Projects Large and Small**	3213
Harvard Business Essentials: **Creating Teams with an Edge**	290X
Harvard Business Essentials: **Entrepreneur's Toolkit**	4368
Harvard Business Essentials: **Coaching and Mentoring**	435X
Harvard Business Essentials: **Crisis Management**	4376
Harvard Business Essentials: **Time Management**	6336
Harvard Business Essentials: **Power, Influence, and Persuasion**	631X
Harvard Business Essentials: **Strategy**	6328
Harvard Business Essentials: **Decision Making**	7618
Harvard Business Essentials: **Marketer's Toolkit**	7626
Harvard Business Essentials: **Performance Management**	9428

To order, call 1-800-668-6780, or go online at www.HBSPress.org

The Results-Driven Manager

The Results-Driven Manager series collects timely articles from *Harvard Management Update* and *Harvard Management Communication Letter* to help senior to middle managers sharpen their skills, increase their effectiveness, and gain a competitive edge. Presented in a concise, accessible format to save managers valuable time, these books offer authoritative insights and techniques for improving job performance and achieving immediate results.

These books are priced at US$14.95
Price subject to change.

Title	Product #
The Results-Driven Manager: **Face-to-Face Communications for Clarity and Impact**	3477
The Results-Driven Manager: **Managing Yourself for the Career You Want**	3469
The Results-Driven Manager: **Presentations That Persuade and Motivate**	3493
The Results-Driven Manager: **Teams That Click**	3507
The Results-Driven Manager: **Winning Negotiations That Preserve Relationships**	3485
The Results-Driven Manager: **Dealing with Difficult People**	6344
The Results-Driven Manager: **Taking Control of Your Time**	6352
The Results-Driven Manager: **Getting People on Board**	6360
The Results-Driven Manager: **Motivating People for Improved Performance**	7790
The Results-Driven Manager: **Becoming an Effective Leader**	7804
The Results-Driven Manager: **Managing Change to Reduce Resistance**	7812
The Results-Driven Manager: **Hiring Smart for Competitive Advantage**	9726
The Results-Driven Manager: **Retaining Your Best People**	9734
The Results-Driven Manager: **Business Etiquette for the New Workplace**	9742

Title	Product #
The Results-Driven Manager:	
Connecting With Your Customers	3234
The Results-Driven Manager:	
Written Communications That Inform and Influence	3226

Management Dilemmas:
Case Studies from the Pages of Harvard Business Review

When facing a difficult management challenge, wouldn't it be great if you could turn to a panel of experts to help guide you to the right decision? Now you can, with books from the Management Dilemmas series. Drawn from the pages of Harvard Business Review, each insightful guide poses a range of familiar and perplexing business situations and shares the wisdom of a small group of leading experts on how each of them would resolve the problem. Engagingly written, these interactive, solutions-oriented collections allow readers to match wits with the experts. They are designed to help managers hone their instincts and problem-solving skills to make sound judgment calls on everyday management dilemmas.

These books are priced at US$19.95
Price subject to change.

Title	Product #
Management Dilemmas: **When Change Comes Undone**	5038
Management Dilemmas: **When Good People Behave Badly**	5046
Management Dilemmas: **When Marketing Becomes a Minefield**	290X
Management Dilemmas: **When People Are the Problem**	7138
Management Dilemmas: **When Your Strategy Stalls**	712X

To order, call 1-800-668-6780, or go online at www.HBSPress.org

How to Order

Harvard Business School Press publications are available worldwide
from your local bookseller or online retailer.
You can also call

1-800-668-6780

Our product consultants are available to help you
8:00 a.m.–6:00 p.m., Monday–Friday, Eastern Time.
Outside the U.S. and Canada, call: 617-783-7450
Please call about special discounts for quantities greater than ten.

You can order online at

www.HBSPress.org